W9-BJT-515

BUENOS AIRES
ENCOUNTER

BRIDGET GLEESON

Buenos Aires Encounter

Published by Lonely Planet Publications Pty Ltd
ABN 36 005 607 983

Australia	Head Office, Locked Bag 1, Footscray, Vic 3011 ☎ 03 8379 8000 fax 03 8379 8111 talk2us@lonelyplanet.com.au
USA	150 Linden St, Oakland, CA 94607 ☎ 510 250 6400 toll free 800 275 8555 fax 510 893 8572 info@lonelyplanet.com
UK	2nd fl, 186 City Rd London EC1V 2NT ☎ 020 7106 2100 fax 020 7106 2101 go@lonelyplanet.co.uk

The first edition was written by Lara Dunston and Terry Carter. This edition was commissioned in Lonely Planet's Oakland office and produced by: **Commissioning Editor** Kathleen Munnelly **Coordinating Editor** Jessica Crouch **Coordinating Cartographer** David Kemp **Layout Designer** Carol Jackson **Assisting Editor** Diana Saad **Managing Editor** Imogen Bannister **Managing Cartographer** David Connolly **Cover Designer** Katy Murenu **Project Manager** Chris Girdler **Managing Layout Designer** Sally Darmody **Thanks to** Glenn Beanland, Lucy Birchley, Jessica Boland, James Hardy, Laura Jane, Alison Lyall, Raphael Richards, Amanda Sierp

ISBN 978 1 74179 287 4

Printed through Colorcraft Ltd, Hong Kong.
Printed in China.

Mixed Sources
Product group from well-managed
forests and other controlled sources
www.fsc.org Cert no. SGS-COC-005002
© 1996 Forest Stewardship Council

HOW TO USE THIS BOOK
Colour-Coding & Maps
Colour-coding is used for symbols on maps and in the text that they relate to (eg all eating venues on the maps and in the text are given a green knife and fork symbol). Each neighborhood also gets its own color, and this is used down the edge of the page and throughout that neighborhood section.

Shaded yellow areas on the maps denote 'areas of interest' — for their historical significance, their attractive architecture or their great bars and restaurants. We encourage you to head to these areas and just start exploring!

Prices
Multiple prices listed with reviews (eg $10/5 or $10/5/20) indicate adult/child, adult/concession or adult/child/family.

Send us your feedback We love to hear from readers — your comments help make our books better. We read every word you send us, and we always guarantee that your feedback goes straight to the appropriate authors. The most useful submissions are rewarded with a free book. To send us your updates and find out about Lonely Planet events, newsletters and travel news visit our award-winning website: **lonelyplanet.com/contact**.

Note: We may edit, reproduce and incorporate your comments in Lonely Planet products such as guidebooks, websites and digital products, so let us know if you don't want your comments reproduced or your name acknowledged. For a copy of our privacy policy visit **lonelyplanet.com/privacy**.

BRIDGET GLEESON

Though born and raised in the US, Bridget hasn't lived in her native country in years. She studied in Rome, taught English in Prague, worked with children in an impoverished community in Nicaragua, and listened to countless stories of her mother's solo adventures through South America in the '70s, before arriving in Argentina at the start of 2007. These days, Bajofondo is on heavy rotation in her apartment in Montserrat and she can (usually) understand porteño (BA local) hyperbole and hand gestures. While trying to detect notes of plum and oak in a glass of Malbec, she's worked as a journalist, editor and sometime photographer for Time Out, National Geographic Personal Explorer, Sherman's Travel and Tablet Hotels. Bridget also photographed many of the images in this book.

BRIDGET'S THANKS

Many thanks to the editors and journalists in Buenos Aires who support me and the porteños who educate me. A special thank you to my family members near and far – especially the one who teaches me how to look at the world through an artistic lens, the one who gives up Saturdays to help me research, and the ones who encouraged me to write and travel in the first place.

THE PHOTOGRAPHER

Terry Carter has photographed several guidebooks for Lonely Planet, including Buenos Aires, where he loves shooting the architectural mishmash of the city despite being constantly told his camera will get stolen.

Our readers Many thanks to the travelers who wrote to us with helpful hints, useful advice and interesting anecdotes. Niels Andersen, Bianca Celestin, Elisabeth Gandolfo, Katharine Gordon, Nina Mikander, Philip Salt, Diana Swartz.

A house in Abasto painted in traditional *filete* (p72) style

CONTENTS

THE AUTHOR	**3**	>ART	147
THIS IS BUENOS AIRES	**7**	>SPORTS	148
HIGHLIGHTS	**8**	>ARCHITECTURE	149
BUENOS AIRES		>BUENOS AIRES	
CALENDAR	**23**	WITH KIDS	150
ITINERARIES	**27**	**BACKGROUND**	**151**
NEIGHBORHOODS	**32**	**DIRECTORY**	**160**
>MICROCENTRO	36	**INDEX**	**170**
>PUERTO MADERO	46		
>CONGRESO &			
TRIBUNALES	52		
>RETIRO	62		
>SAN TELMO	70		
>LA BOCA	84		
>RECOLETA & BARRIO			
NORTE	90		
>PALERMO	102		
>PALERMO VIEJO	112		
>LAS CAÑITAS &			
BELGRANO	128		
SNAPSHOTS			
>ACCOMMODATIONS	136		
>TANGO	138		
>MUSIC	140		
>FOOD	141		
>BARS	142		
>CLUBS	143		
>GAY & LESBIAN BA	144		
>FASHION	145		
>ESTANCIAS	146		

THIS IS BUENOS AIRES

Buenos Aires runs on nostalgia and cosmopolitan ambition. For every group of trendsetters laughing over cocktails, there's a cluster of old-timers gathered around a radio, a tear rolling down someone's cheek as Carlos Gardel sings of the glowing street lamps of his beloved city.

The dichotomy is rooted in Argentina's tumultuous past. The capital city, once a prosperous European-style metropolis teeming with glamorous tango halls and grand cafes, buckled under the strain of a military government and several economic collapses. But Buenos Aires is back on its feet. A talented generation of designers, *fútbolistas* (soccer players), musicians and restaurateurs have reinvigorated the beleaguered capital, transforming it into one of the most talked-about travel destinations on the planet.

The hype, after all, is warranted – the steak really is the best in the world, dance halls fill with tango students every night of the week, the soccer matches are intense and passionate, the wine is affordable and delicious. But Buenos Aires' magnetism, as any porteño (BA local) will tell you, extends well beyond such clichés. Architecturally speaking, the city is a fascinating microcosm of styles from colonial to belle epoque to modernist. The Parisian-style cafe circuit, backed by an intriguing literary history, is paradise for bookish types and coffee lovers, and the edgy local fashion scene seduces design-minded travelers.

Gorge yourself on red meat at a rustic *parrilla* (grill restaurant), nurse a bottle of Malbec at an old-fashioned *milonga* (social dance) as local tango dancers embrace dramatically on the wooden dance floor, pull an all-nighter at a thumping electronic venues along the Costanera, revel in gaucho culture at a *peña* (folk music club). Give Buenos Aires some time. Soon you'll begin to understand the bittersweet charm – the poignant collision of old-fashioned sensibility and contemporary revolution – that simultaneously thrills visitors and makes old men shed a tear or two.

Left *Hola* from a junior *fútbolista* (soccer player) and friends above the Caminito, La Boca (p86)

>1 Learn to tango in an old-fashioned dance hall 10
>2 Honor the dearly departed at the Recoleta Cemetery 11
>3 Catch *fútbol* fever at La Bombonera stadium 12
>4 Wander the streets of quaint and crumbling San Telmo 13
>5 Sip cappuccino at one of the city's classic cafes 14
>6 Shop till you drop at the city's open-air fairs 15
>7 Taste-test wines from Argentina's best bodegas 16
>8 Pay tribute to Las Madres in Plaza de Mayo 17
>9 Contemplate fine art and industry at La Boca's Fundación Proa 18
>10 Join the hoedown at a country-style *peña* 19
>11 Retreat to a leafy urban oasis 20
>12 Get down with gauchos 21
>13 Dig into juicy steak at a *parrilla* 22

The music at the Feria San Pedro Telmo (p73) will put you in the mood for tango

>1 MILONGAS
LEARN TO TANGO IN AN OLD-FASHIONED DANCE HALL

Sensuous and melancholy, the tango is quintessentially porteño (BA local). Though the dance form was born in the brothels of Buenos Aires' poor immigrant barrios, its humble roots are often hidden beneath champagne and glitter at tourist-oriented tango shows. For a more authentic taste of tango, flee the tour-bus masses and dart through the shadows to a *milonga* (social dance). Here you'll find locals of all ages – some in fishnets, others in jeans – acting out human drama and seduction on the dance floor.

Start at Confitería Ideal (p45), a historic downtown cafe with a grand ballroom on the upper level. Antique chandeliers and marble pillars evoke old-world elegance, and the faded velvet and tango orchestras add a certain dusty charm that draws a nightly crowd of experienced local dancers. Classes are held before the *milonga* for the regulars begins at 11pm.

Once you know the difference between Gardel and Piazzolla, take your dancing shoes over to El Beso (p60) or the Centro Region Leonesa (p61; pictured above). Both venues host classes before dimming the lights for a *milonga*. Too shy to wrap your arms (and legs) around a stranger? Just order a glass of wine and watch the city's skilled *tangueros* do their thing. But don't stare too long at the handsome stranger across the room – an open gaze, according to *milonga* etiquette, is an invitation to dance.

For more on tango, see p138.

>2 CEMENTERIO DE LA RECOLETA
HONOR THE DEARLY DEPARTED AT THE RECOLETA CEMETERY

Pay your respects to the city's late and great at the spectacular Cementerio de la Recoleta, a necropolis ornate enough to rival Père Lachaise in Paris or the above-ground cities of the dead in New Orleans.

Occupying almost 55,000 sq meters in the center of Recoleta, the cemetery was consecrated in 1882 as Buenos Aires' first public burial ground. Like the surrounding neighborhood, the graveyard quickly grew exclusive – today it's crowded with 4800 tombs holding the remains of the city's most famous families. Among the noteworthy names buried here are 19th-century president Domingo Sarmiento, twice-president Hipólito Yrigoyen, boxing legend Luis Angel Firpo (aka 'the wild bull of the pampas') and, of course, Eva Perón. But don't expect a grandiose monument to the former first lady. Evita's remains are contained in a simple black granite vault in a plot marked by her family name, Duarte.

The appeal of the cemetery goes well beyond the fame of its permanent residents – the intriguing site is a maze of narrow passageways lined with crumbling marble statuary and decorative mausoleums in architectural styles from art nouveau to neo-Gothic. Follow a stray cat through the alleys to discover cherubs in stone relief, stained-glass windows edged with cobwebs, marble angels and bittersweet poetry etched into granite.

See p93 for more information.

>3 LA BOMBONERA STADIUM

CATCH FÚTBOL FEVER AT LA BOMBONERA STADIUM

In Buenos Aires, *fútbol* is not just a game. The national pastime inspires near-religious passion in porteños, clearing the city streets and sending spectators into fits of ecstasy and anguish as they huddle around TV screens or brave the explosive stadium crowds. Witnessing a match at La Bombonera, the famed stadium of Club Atlético Boca Juniors, is an unforgettable experience. But don't brave the volatile masses alone – unless you're going to the game with a streetwise native, it's best to book tickets through a tour operator (see p89).

The city's rival teams symbolize distinct factions of porteño demography. Club Atlético River Plate (known simply as 'River') hails from the affluent north side, while Boca Juniors proudly represents the blue-collar south. La Bombonera, fittingly enough for Boca's home turf, sits smack in the center of one of the city's roughest barrios. Fifty-five thousand frenzied fans take to the stands on Sunday afternoons for two hours of drama; the stadium hums and vibrates as loyal supporters jump in time to rhythmic drum beats and scream at the officials.

The atmosphere is particularly boisterous (read – out of control) when River and Boca face off during the much-anticipated Super-clásico match. Choose between *los millonarios* (the millionaires) and the working-class heroes, then let the games begin – just be sure to dodge the scuffles that inevitably break out in the parking lot.

See also p89.

>4 SAN TELMO

WANDER THE STREETS OF QUAINT AND CRUMBLING SAN TELMO

The barrio of San Telmo exudes faded grandeur and bohemian spirit. The neighborhood's elegant belle-epoque architecture and crumbling villas are throwbacks to the district's 19th-century heyday. Before yellow fever and cholera sent the beau monde fleeing for higher ground, aristocratic Spanish families traversed the cobblestone streets in horse-drawn carriages.

After the epidemic, San Telmo's poor immigrants turned abandoned mansions into makeshift homes and the neighborhood quickly fell into disrepair. The pretty barrio has exuded an unpretentious, working-class charm ever since, with antique dealers, tango clubs and restaurants drawing a steady stream of tourists and locals in recent years. The heart of the neighborhood, the Spanish-style Plaza Dorrego (p73), bustles daily with street performers, hippie artisans, beer-swilling backpackers and a clumsy (but occasionally successful) band of local pickpockets.

Wander along Defensa (pictured above) or Balcarce towards the leafy Parque Lezama (p72) and take in the picturesque vista of romantic facades, climbing vines and drooping balconies. After touring El Zanjón de Granados (p72), a colonial mansion that reveals the neighborhood's history, stop into the Mercado de San Telmo (p75) to poke through antique spoons and pick up fresh fruit and cheese for a picnic. Current gentrification efforts may be changing the barrio's character, but the appeal of San Telmo's old-fashioned corner cafes and rustic *parrillas*, thankfully, remains alive and kicking.

See also p70.

>5 CAFE CULTURE

SIP CAPPUCCINO AT ONE OF THE CITY'S CLASSIC CAFES

Good news for francophiles, bookworms and travelers who refuse to talk until they've had their morning caffeine jolt: Buenos Aires isn't called the Paris of the south for nothing. In addition to the grand boulevards and art-nouveau architecture that invite comparisons with the French capital, BA's lively cafe culture emanates Parisian appeal.

Once havens for famous writers like Jorge Luis Borges (see p68) and Spanish playwright Federico García Lorca, downtown cafes remain integral to daily life in Buenos Aires. Get your coffee fix with a *café con leche y medialunas* (cafe latte and croissants) and linger in one of the old-fashioned spaces. Here formally dressed waiters serve porteños from all walks of life, tango paraphernalia and old photographs cover the walls, and large picture windows frame the activity on busy sidewalks outside.

Embark on a cafe itinerary: start at atmospheric 36 Billares (p59), García Lorca's cafe of choice, then move on to Café Tortoni (p43), the city's oldest cafe. Opened in 1858, Tortoni was a regular haunt of the legendary tango singer Carlos Gardel (p56). The flash of tourists' cameras doesn't stop office workers from dropping in for a *cafecito* (small espresso). Ask for a *café cortado* (espresso shot with a little milk) with *churros* (fried, sweet pastries) and absorb the historic atmosphere before finishing the circuit at the stately Café Richmond (p43; pictured above), the one-time meeting place of Borges and his writer pals.

>6 ARTISAN FAIRS

SHOP TILL YOU DROP AT THE CITY'S OPEN-AIR FAIRS

The sun is shining, the silver is gleaming and pesos are burning a hole in your pocket – there's nothing like an artisan fair on a Sunday morning. On weekends, Buenos Aires' outdoor markets surge with treasure-hunters snapping up everything from antique teapots and Mapuche-inspired silver jewelry to cashmere sweaters and handmade leather boots. Forget economic tensions – this is a shopaholic's playground.

Antique lovers make a beeline for the grandfather of Sunday fairs, the Feria San Pedro Telmo (p73). The main drag, Defensa, throngs with people browsing through cobalt-blue antique seltzer bottles and vintage sunglasses while tango orchestras play in the street (just how did that guy move his piano down his apartment's staircase and across San Telmo's cobblestones?) When the sun sets, an evening *milonga* starts in Plaza Dorrego (p73).

An array of artisan creations from hammered bronze rings to hand-woven leather sandals stock the stalls at the designer market on Recoleta's Plaza Francia (p96; pictured above). Vendors sell sandwiches piled high with slabs of salami and cheese while musical acts play for a barefoot crowd on the grassy slope. Further north, the designer markets skirting Palermo Viejo's Plaza Serrano teem with porteño hipsters scouring the racks for military-style jackets and graphic T-shirts. Don't have much room in your suitcase? Pick up a pair of brightly patterned underthings, a perennial hit with the locals.

See also p145.

>7 ARGENTINE WINE

TASTE-TEST WINES FROM ARGENTINA'S BEST BODEGAS

Wine connoisseurs raise their glasses to Argentina, one of the world's premium producers. The industry centers around the Mendoza province, where a sunny, dry climate creates ideal growing conditions; popular grapes include Malbec, which produces a medium-bodied red, and the indigenous Torrontés, the basis for an aromatic white varietal.

Rather than holing up in your hotel room with a bottle of red, appreciate Argentina's impressive wines by attending an educational tasting. Nigel Tollerman, the friendly British proprietor of the wine delivery service 0800-Vino and the sommelier at Francis Ford Coppola's new Buenos Aires hotel, offers casual tastings at his small cellar in Abasto (p108; pictured above). The informal lesson includes an 'aromas kit,' an assortment of cheeses and some hard-to-find special edition wines. More structured tastings with a gourmet food pairing option are run by Anuva Vinos (p130), a wine club that exports carefully selected bottles to the US and Europe. American expat Daniel Karlin conducts tastings at upscale restaurants and, on request, he'll hold a private tasting at your hotel. The poshest wine tasting in Buenos Aires occurs in the elegant cellar at the Alvear Palace Hotel's La Bourgogne restaurant (p98). The knowledgeable sommelier pours varietals and talks tannins while a tuxedoed waiter brings around bite-sized cuisine from the corresponding regions.

>8 PLAZA DE MAYO

PAY TRIBUTE TO LAS MADRES IN PLAZA DE MAYO

Founded in 1580, Plaza de Mayo is a stage on which many of the dramatic events in Argentina's modern history have played out. The central plaza saw massive trade union demonstrations and Eva Perón shouting from Casa Rosada's lower balcony in 1945, military bombings in 1955, and the police shooting of five protestors during the 2001 economic crisis. The pigeon-populated square hosts demonstrations and rallies most days of the week, but the peaceful Thursday vigil of Las Madres de Plaza de Mayo (Mothers of the Plaza de Mayo) is the most powerful and touching.

Since 1977, the Madres have demonstrated against the military-ordered kidnapping, torture and execution of up to 30,000 people during the 1976–83 'Dirty War.' In memory of their 'disappeared' children and family members, the Madres founded a formal organization to search for the missing, donning symbolic white headscarves and coordinating regular marches demanding justice.

Although in 1986 the Madres split into factions – one focused on locating remains and seeking justice, the other widening their mission to support other causes of injustice – the much-admired mothers came together on April 30, 2007 for a 30th anniversary concert celebrating their courage. Support the cause by stopping by the Madres' bookshop and cafe (p58).

See also p40.

>9 LA BOCA

CONTEMPLATE FINE ART AND INDUSTRY AT LA BOCA'S FUNDACIÓN PROA

You'll do a triple take when you first glimpse the sleek Fundación Proa rising, stately and silver, above the filthy river and broken-down buildings of La Boca. The city's most distinguished art gallery is in fine form after an extensive renovation. Now Proa is a standout, not only for its clout in the international art scene – a Marcel Duchamp exhibit heralded the reopening – but also for its unlikely location in a recycled building on La Boca's gritty riverfront, miles away from the gallery districts of Recoleta and Palermo.

Thanks to Proa and its fashionable terrace cafe, La Boca is again worth a full afternoon's excursion. The barrio, once the city's principal port, owes its vibrant appearance to the Italian immigrants who spruced up their corrugated tin homes with boldly colored paints. Today's tourists swarm Caminito (Little Walkway) and the historic rainbow of houses while professional tango dancers twirl in the street in homage to the dance form that originated here. While the block is visually appealing, it can also feel like a tourist trap filled with second-rate souvenir shops and leather hustlers. Take the obligatory stroll through the historic quarter before you head to Proa, where you can gape at the Riachuelo through the spotless glass panes. Note that the rough-and-tumble barrio has the city's highest crime rate; catch the bus or a taxi back towards the center.

See also p86 and p86.

>10 LA PEÑA DEL COLORADO

JOIN THE HOEDOWN AT A COUNTRY-STYLE PEÑA

Don't cry into your *cerveza* (beer) if you don't have enough time to spend the day at a country *estancia* (ranch) or visit the suburban Feria de Mataderos (p58) – you can soak up some gaucho culture without leaving the city limits. *Peñas* are folkloric music clubs where regional musicians perform on stage and a jovial crowd chows down on country-style cuisine. After the set, the real festivities commence as the audience passes around harmonicas and *charangos* (five-stringed guitars) for a community jam session.

Rustic, traditional and generally little-known to tourists, *peñas* are scattered about the city. Access the cowboy subculture at Palermo's friendly La Peña del Colorado (p111; pictured above). A country kitchen serves up a full menu of classic dishes from the far reaches of Argentina – Patagonian lamb and *tamales* (steamed cornmeal stuffed with meat and cheese) from the northern province of Tucumán, gnocchi stuffed with cassava grown by the Guaraní tribe – alongside *mate* (a local tea) and Argentine wines. Rotating musical offerings include vocalists from Jujuy province singing old-fashioned laments, Uruguayan guitarists and youthful folk ensembles featuring percussion and wind instruments.

On weekend nights, the *peña* packs in visiting cowboys, gaucho wannabes, eager tourists and stressed-out city dwellers looking to unwind. Get into the mood with free-flowing, sticky sweet *patero* wine – it'll help you work up the courage to grab a harmonica and join the country hoedown at the end of the night.

>11 CITY PARKS
RETREAT TO A LEAFY URBAN OASIS

Even the most cosmopolitan traveler needs an occasional escape from the traffic-choked streets of downtown Buenos Aires. Throw together a picnic lunch – a half dozen *empanadas* (savory-filled pastries) and a mini bottle of Malbec should do the trick – and retire to one of the city's green spaces for a lazy afternoon. You'll feel wonderfully indulgent drinking wine on the grass while fitness-conscious porteños scamper past in shiny workout garb.

On the north side of the city, the sprawling Parque 3 de Febrero (p107) is your best bet for alfresco revelry. The one-time private retreat of 19th-century dictator Juan Manuel de Rosas is now a verdant playground for porteños of all persuasions: families cruising the artificial lake on candy-colored pedal boats, muscled men rolling by on in-line skates, couples kissing in the rose gardens, dreadlocked kids strumming guitars and elderly folk passing around *mate* gourds. For more exotic wildlife, check out the gargantuan koi fish at the nearby Jardín Japonés (p104) and the roaming peacocks at the Jardín Zoológico (p104).

Further south, the Reserva Ecológica (p49) is the riverside refuge of choice. Do as the locals do – pick up a couple of sandwiches, such as a *choripan* (a sausage sandwich) or *bondiola* (piled high with grilled steak) at one of the *parrilla* carts near the entrance, then rent a rusty set of wheels at the adjacent bicycle stand and pedal into the reserve for a picnic near the water.

HIGHLIGHTS

>12 LA FERIA DE MATADEROS

GET DOWN WITH GAUCHOS

Folk music emanates from the outdoor stage, local couples take to the streets to perform the traditional *chacarera* and *chamamé* folk dances, food stalls dish out hearty country dishes like *locro* (a meaty stew from northwest Argentina), deep-fried *empanadas*, and *humitas* (lightly sweetened corn meal wrapped in corn husks), all washed down with sweet *patero* wine – this is La Feria de Mataderos, an authentic celebration of Argentine country traditions.

This lively festival and market is held every weekend (except during the summer) in Mataderos, the western Buenos Aires suburb named for the cattle slaughterhouses established there in 1899. While the stage features children twirling in vibrantly colored skirts and adolescent boys performing gallant folk dances in traditional boots and *bombachas* (loose-fitting gaucho-style trousers), the most exciting spectacle of the day is the *sortija*. In full gaucho regalia, horsemen stand on their saddles and ride at full speed to spear a tiny ring dangling from a ribbon.

After you've marveled at the horses and gorged yourself on country cuisine, stroll through the market for bargain-priced leather goods, ponchos and silver jewelry. A row of gourmet food stands offer samples of homemade cheeses and decadent *dulce de leche* liqueur.

See also p58.

>13 ARGENTINE BEEF

DIG INTO JUICY STEAK AT A PARRILLA

Believe the hype: Argentine beef is the best in the world. Eat, drink and be merry at one of Buenos Aires' numerous *parrillas* (grill restaurants), where a leisurely steak dinner begins with waiters pouring Malbec and carving generous slabs of rare prime beef. *Parrillas* run the range from down-to-earth neighborhood joints like La Dorita (p120) and Desnivel (p77), popular spots for inexpensive but traditional grilled specialties, to classic establishments like the refined Don Julio (p120) and stylish steakhouses like Miranda (p121), a favorite of Palermo's fashion-conscious carnivores.

Why is Argentine beef so special? It's the happy cows fattening up on nutritious pampas grass rather than corn and growth hormones. As the meat's primarily produced for export, the leaner, more natural-tasting beef you'll try here is generally not aged, which contributes to its distinct flavor. Another key factor is that Argentine ranchers have kept strict control over breeding, crossing European with British stock to create high-quality and mostly free-range beef.

A *parrillada* (mixed grill) is the meat-eater's litmus test: besides cuts of beef, it almost invariably includes delicacies such as *chinchulines* (intestines), *morcilla* (blood sausage) and *chorizo* (sausage). Sizzling *provoleta* (grilled provolone cheese) and red wine round out the meat-lover's fantasy.

>BUENOS AIRES CALENDAR

There's always something happening in Buenos Aires. The only time the streets are calm, in fact, is during major *fútbol* (soccer) matches, when locals huddle around their TV sets, and during the sweltering Christmas holidays when half the population decamps to the beach. The cultural calendar has long revolved around traditional pastimes like tango and horses, but the continued growth of the dynamic fine arts scene has brought a host of fashion, music and art events to Buenos Aires' annual schedule. Check out the all-inclusive agenda at www .bue.gov.ar to find out what's on while you're in town.

Carlos Gardel (p56), legendary tango crooner and local hero

JANUARY & FEBRUARY

Carnaval

OK, OK, it's a far cry from Rio. But Buenos Aires' Carnaval is fun and lighthearted (though perhaps not for locals stuck in traffic jams as colorful parades shut down a different street every day). Expect to be sprayed with canned foam as ebullient *murga* (dance) troupes dance and drum around Plaza de Mayo.

Chinese New Year

Buenos Aires' bite-sized Chinatown (p130) only spans a few blocks in Belgrano, but what it lacks in floor space it makes up for with enthusiasm on the first day of the Chinese New Year. Exact dates depend on the lunar calendar.

Nuestros Caballos at La Rural

MARCH

Nuestros Caballos

www.nuestroscaballos.com.ar, in Spanish
Argentine horse-lovers gather at Palermo's La Rural (p104) in late March for this all-things-equine exhibition. Expect horse events, produce stalls, and ponchos and gauchos galore.

APRIL

Feria del Libro

www.el-libro.org.ar, in Spanish
Latin American literature is as strong as ever, with over one million book lovers converging on its most important book fair featuring book reading and signing sessions by famous authors from around the world.

Festival Internacional de Cine Independiente

www.bafici.gov.ar, in Spanish
Mid- to late April's excellent independent film festival highlights Argentine, Latin American and international independent films. The main screening venue is at Abasto mall (p108).

MAY

arteBA

www.arteba.com
Held over five days in mid-May at Palermo's La Rural (p104), this event features exhibitions

from hundreds of art galleries and organizations in Buenos Aires, with both national and international contemporary art on display, as well as presentations and discussions.

JUNE

Día de la Muerte de Carlos Gardel

June 24 marks the anniversary of this iconic tango singer's (p56) death. Numerous tango events during the week conclude with a pilgrimage to the Cementerio de la Chacarita, where thousands of fans, some of whom weren't even born when he died, crowd the streets and leave flowers at his tomb.

JULY

La Rural

www.ruralarg.org.ar, in Spanish
Livestock lovers and gaucho groupies will go crazy at this event in July and August, where prize cows (of course), sheep, goats and horses are on display, along with wild gaucho shows and just about everything agricultural. It takes place at Palermo's La Rural (p104). Gaucho *bombachas* (pants) optional.

AUGUST

Fashion Buenos Aires

www.bafweek.com, in Spanish
Rose-colored champagne flows freely, fashionistas chat on iPhones and coltish

teenagers take to the runway – it must be Buenos Aires' biannual fashion week (BAFWeek). For five action-packed days, the finest local designers strut their stuff at Palermo's La Rural (p104).

Tango Buenos Aires

www.festivaldetango.gob.ar, in Spanish
This tango festival has legs wrapping all over the city. The performances offer a great way to see some of the country's best *tanguistas* (female tango dancers) do their thing. Venues include the Centro Cultural Recoleta (p93).

SEPTEMBER

La Semana del Arte en Buenos Aires

www.lasemanadelarte.com.ar, in Spanish
For one week in mid-September, nearly every art gallery and cultural institution in the city opens its doors for a mega-event that highlights some of the best contemporary artists in the country. All forms of media – from photography to video installations and performance art – are represented.

Feria de Vinos y Bodegas

www.argentinewines.com, in Spanish
This sprawling wine fair sees representatives from 250 bodegas decanting wines and talking shop – heaven for lovers of fine Cabernet.

Fiesta del Inmigrante

www.fiestadelinmigrante.com.ar

Practically everyone in Buenos Aires is an immigrant – even if once or twice removed. This joyful weeklong festival honors the locals' ambitious ancestors and features ethnic food, music and dance at the Museo de la Inmigración in Puerto Madero (p48).

OCTOBER

Casa FOA

www.casafoa.com

This innovative design fair serves two purposes: first, to preserve and renovate a landmark structure, and second, to display the cutting-edge work of local architects, designers and landscapers. The venue changes each year; the festival usually runs from October to December.

NOVEMBER

Marcha del Orgullo Gay

www.marchadelorgullo.org.ar, in Spanish

Over 20,000 of BA's gay, lesbian, transgender and bi community march from Plaza de Mayo to the Congreso on the first Saturday in November, and the colorful party gets bigger each year.

Creamfields Buenos Aires

www.creamfieldsba.com

Over 60,000 excited dance music fans dance for 16 hours straight (how *do* they manage that, we wonder?) at one of the world's biggest electronic music festivals.

DECEMBER

Campeonato Abierto Argentino de Polo

www.aapolo.com, in Spanish

Palermo's dedicated polo arena, Campo Argentino de Polo (p133), is the venue for this, the highlight of the spring polo and people-watching season.

Christmas & New Year

These holidays are definitely a family affair in Buenos Aires – but 'family-oriented' doesn't necessarily mean 'wholesome' in this case. These are the days of the year when porteños (BA locals) are, believe it or not, likely to drink too much champagne. The illegal fireworks displays at midnight can be a little dangerous – it's best to watch from a rooftop terrace.

The iconic Obelisco (p40) pierces the sky

ITINERARIES

ONE DAY

Short on time? Start a marathon day with an alfresco caffeine jolt at La Biela (p99), then venture into the Cementerio de la Recoleta (p93). Take a taxi to elegant Av de Mayo to stare at grand architecture and pop into literary coffeehouse Café Tortoni (p43). Take some obligatory photos at Casa Rosada (p38), then hang a right at Defensa and venture into San Telmo. Tuck into a juicy steak at Gran Parrilla del Plata (p77) and poke through the antiques at Mercado de San Telmo (p75). Watch tango dancers while sitting outside at the historic Bar Plaza Dorrego (p79). Can't get enough tango? Attend a slick dinner show at El Querandí (p83) or observe from the sidelines at a *milonga* (social dance) at Confitería Ideal (p45).

THREE DAYS

Check the one-day itinerary off your to-do list, then kick off day two at MALBA (p105). Lunch at Freud y Fahler (p120), then shop for stylish threads in the boutiques around Plaza Serrano. Take a coffee break at the New York–style Mark's Deli (p124), then dine with Palermo Viejo's pretty people at Miranda (p121). Switch from big-city cool to country charm with live gaucho music at Peña del Colorado (p111).

On day three, head to La Boca (p84) for art and coffee on the terrace at Fundación Proa (p86). Amble through El Caminito (p86) before returning to Recoleta for lunch at 788 Food Bar (p98) and a stop in the glamorous El Ateneo Grand Splendid bookshop (p95). Stroll down ritzy Av Alvear and take afternoon tea at L'Orangerie (p97) before feasting on fresh fish at Oviedo (p98).

FIVE DAYS

Put the three-day itinerary behind you before you head over to Puerto Madero to see the antique sailing vessels and Museo Fortabat (p48). Gobble a steak sandwich outside the Ecological Reserve (p49), then pedal towards the river beaches on a rental bike. Go all out for dinner at El Bistro (p50). On day five, pay your respects to Argentina's iconic

---

Top left Soul Café (p132) **Top right** Statue in front of Casa Rosada (p38) **Bottom** Jardín Botánico Carlos Thays (p104)

FORWARD PLANNING

Three weeks ahead A little forethought will make the difference between a pleasant vacation and a cultural experience you'll be talking about for years to come. First, purchase travel insurance and ditch the conspicuous money belt – Buenos Aires' eager pickpockets will snatch it before you know what's hit you. Plan to be in the city during the weekend for San Telmo's antiques fair (p73) and the Feria de Mataderos (p58). Log onto www .whatsupbuenosaires.com, a cool bilingual portal listing cultural happenings from art shows to music festivals, to sign up for event reminders.

One week ahead Snap up tickets for musical acts and theatre at www.ticketek.com.ar, and, if you're planning to go to a *fútbol* match, book ahead with a tour operator like **Tangol** (www.tangol.com.ar). This tourist agency also rents out cell phones and laptop computers, to help travelers stay in touch with their parties and make dinner reservations. See p167 for more info on organized tours.

former first lady at Museo Evita (p106) before exploring Palermo Woods (p107) in the afternoon and knocking back a few frozen mojitos at Milión (p99) at night.

RAINY DAY

Don't blame it on the rain – there's plenty to do in Buenos Aires when the weather turns stormy. Cafe-hop through downtown venues with literary history (p14) and pop into the Museo Xul Solar (p94) before catching an Argentine flick at the Abasto (p108) or Alto Palermo (p107) cinemas. Get lost in the antique stores of San Telmo (see the boxed text, p74) or attend a champagne-soaked opening at an art gallery (see the boxed text, p94). Linger over a rich meal, then settle in for some jazz at cozy Thelonious Club (p111).

UP ALL NIGHT

This city doesn't sleep. Porteños go out late, stay out late, and rise late. Take a disco nap in the early evening before dining at Gran Bar Danzon (p98) – the busy late-night eatery has a bar where you can continue the party after dessert. Move on to Las Cañitas around midnight for microbrews at Van Koning (p132) or retro cocktails at Soul Café and Supersoul (p132). Hit the clubs after 2am – try cool Niceto Club (p127) or the rollicking venues along the Costanera Norte (p122). Breakfast at Bar 6 (p123) or, on a Sunday, the popular Scandinavian-style brunch at Ølsen (p121).

Enjoy a Scandinavian brunch at Ølsen (p121), Palermo Viejo

BUDGET BA

Just because you can't afford drinks at the Faena (p51) doesn't mean your vacation's a bust – many of the city's delights are either inexpensive or free. There's no admission price to check out edgy art at the Centro Cultural Recoleta (p93), and MALBA (p105) is free on Wednesdays. Tango performances in Plaza Dorrego (p73) or along El Caminito (p86) won't cost you a penny; entrance to parks like the Jardín Botánico (p104) are also gratis. How to dine on the cheap? Look for affordable *menus ejecutivos* (set-lunch menus) or head to a budget-friendly San Telmo steakhouse like La Vieja Rotisería (p77). If all else fails, a box of freshly baked *empanadas* (savory-filled pastries) only costs a handful of pesos.

>NEIGHBORHOODS

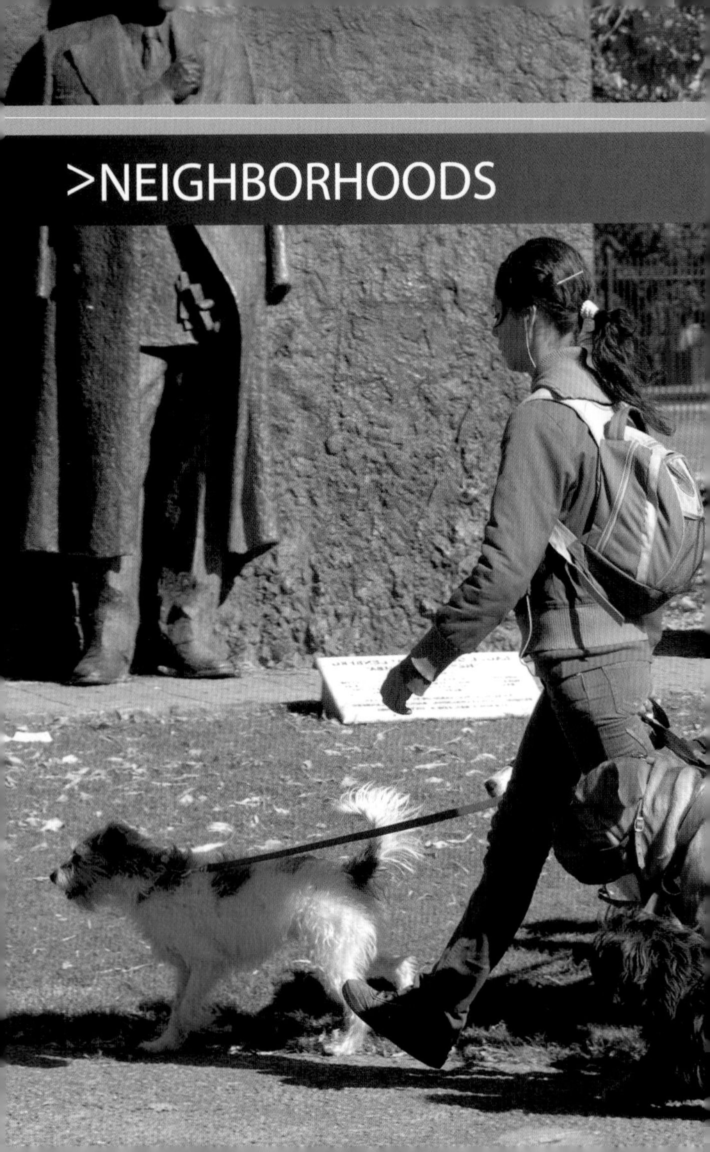

>1	Microcentro	36
>2	Puerto Madero	46
>3	Congreso & Tribunales	52
>4	Retiro	62
>5	San Telmo	70
>6	La Boca	84
>7	Recoleta & Barrio Norte	90
>8	Palermo	102
>9	Palermo Viejo	112
>10	Las Cañitas & Belgrano	128

A day at the office for a dog walker in one of Palermo's parks (p20)

NEIGHBORHOODS

A grand downtown, a sleek city harbor, a working-class quarter quickly gentrifying, a bohemian enclave turned fashion district – the ever-changing barrios of Buenos Aires are as colorful as a tango dancer's wardrobe and as diverse as the profanities spewed forth by the city's fervent *fútbol* fans.

The urban geography isn't complex if you break it down like the locals do: most porteños (BA locals), consciously or not, divide their hometown into north and south. The former, to generalize, is affluent, clean and contemporary, while the latter is Buenos Aires' historic center and home to the city's most staggeringly beautiful architecture.

But how to decipher this north/south divide? A simple history lesson: the southern neighborhoods were the original stomping grounds of European immigrants who arrived in Buenos Aires at the end of the 18th century. Poor Italians settled near the port of La Boca, and the barrio's been vibrant but run-down ever since. Wealthy Spaniards threw lavish parties and drank wine in the villas of San Telmo until a yellow fever epidemic drove them out of the barrio in 1871. The neighborhood took on a distinct blue-collar feel until recent restoration efforts unveiled the grandeur beneath San Telmo's tattered exterior. Meanwhile, Congreso still features the visually spectacular Av de Mayo, the legacy of creative European architects, and Puerto Madero, the port that once welcomed immigrants into the city, has been redesigned to resemble a stylish London-style harbor.

The rich Spaniards headed north when disease struck San Telmo, and the rest is history. Recoleta became their new outpost – as evidenced by the French-style architecture and aristocrats who still live there today – and you can see money everywhere in the upscale barrios of Palermo Viejo, Belgrano and Las Cañitas. The Microcentro, Buenos Aires' buzzing business district, bridges the gap between north and south. But don't choose between fashion and history – you'll spend plenty of time feasting on red meat and sightseeing on both sides of town.

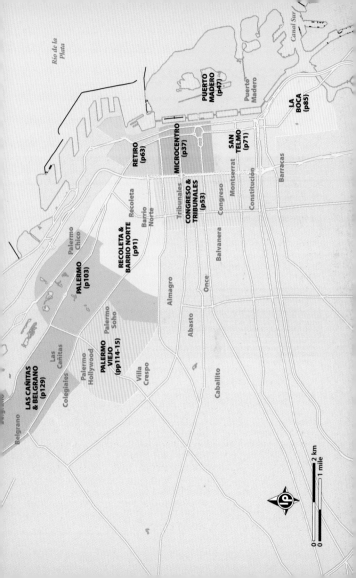

Río de la Plata

Canal Sur

PUERTO MADERO (p47)

Puerto Madero

LA BOCA (p85)

RETIRO (p63)

MICROCENTRO (p37)

SAN TELMO (p71)

Tribunales

CONGRESO & TRIBUNALES (p53)

Recoleta

Barrio Norte

Montserrat

Congreso

Constitución

Barracas

RECOLETA & BARRIO NORTE (p91)

Palermo Chico

Balvanera

PALERMO (p103)

Almagro

Once

Palermo Soho

Abasto

PALERMO VIEJO (pp114–15)

Caballito

Palermo Hollywood

Villa Crespo

Las Cañitas

LAS CAÑITAS & BELGRANO (p129)

Colegiales

Belgrano

0   2 km
0   1 mile

>MICROCENTRO

If you suddenly find yourself surrounded by handsome men in spiffy three-piece suits, you'll know you've made it to the Microcentro. The administrative, business and commercial center of the city surges with an energetic crowd during the day – priests filing into the Catedral Metropolitana, investment bankers shouting into their cell phones, free-spirited artisans selling jewelry behind the Cabildo, the Madres marching in protest around the central square and college students highlighting their textbooks in coffee shops. Plaza de Mayo, sitting at the heart of the neighborhood, sees a rally or demonstration almost every day, while traffic-free shopping thoroughfares Florida and Lavalle swarm with on-the-go businessmen and tourists haggling with salesmen over the price of leather jackets. The Microcentro is notoriously hectic, but recent endeavors to pedestrianize more city streets are making the business district more user-friendly – and braving the diverse downtown crowd is all part of the local experience.

MICROCENTRO

◉ SEE
Cabildo de Buenos
  Aires 1 B5
Casa de la Cultura 2 B5
Casa Rosada 3 C5
Catedral Metropolitana 4 C4
Centro Cultural Borges ..5 B2
Galería Güemes 6 B4
Iglesia Santa Catalina ...7 B2
Manzana de las Luces 8 B5
Museo Etnográfico 9 C5
Obelisco 10 A3
Plaza de Mayo 11 C5

⬚ SHOP
Darcos Tango 12 A3
Galerías Pacífico 13 B2

Plata Nativa 14 B2
Prüne 15 B3
Winery 16 B4

🍴 EAT
Brasserie Berry 17 B3
California Burrito
  Company 18 B3
Casa Roca 19 B3
D'oro 20 B5
Pura Vida 21 C3
Tomo1 ....22 A3

🍸 DRINK
Café Richmond 23 B3
Café Tortoni 24 A5
La Cigale 25 C2

La Puerto Rico 26 C5
Le Bar 27 C3

⭐ PLAY
Bahrein 28 C3
Big One 29 A5
Cocoliche 30 A5
Confitería Ideal 31 A5
Luna Park 32 D3
Teatro Gran Rex 33 A3

👁 SEE

📷 CABILDO DE BUENOS AIRES

☎ 4342-6729; Bolívar 65, Microcentro; admission $1; 🕐 museum 11:30am-6pm Tue-Fri, 2-6pm Sat & Sun; Ⓜ Line A Perú, Line D Catedral, Line E Bolívar; ♿

The pristine white Cabildo was the seat of the Spanish-run city government from 1580 to 1821. Today's colonial-style structure is a testament to haphazard city planning: the original Cabildo was supported by 11 arches that spanned Av de Mayo, but six were demolished to make room for new avenues. A small museum inside houses historical artifacts, and on Thursdays and Fridays an artisan fair takes over the courtyard.

📷 CASA DE LA CULTURA

☎ 4323-9669; Av de Mayo 575, Microcentro; admission free; 🕐 8am-8pm Mon-Fri, closed Jan; Ⓜ Line A Perú, Line D Catedral, Line E Bolívar

Before the internet, apparently, there was glamour in the newsroom. Step through the huge cast-iron doors of the Casa de la Cultura (Office of Culture) into a vestige of the golden age of newspaper journalism. The lobby's dark-wood kiosks and a display of old-fashioned printing equipment hark back to the days when the building was the headquarters of the daily La Prensa newspaper.

📷 CASA ROSADA

☎ 4344-3802; www.museo.gov.ar, in Spanish; Hipólito Yrigoyen 219, Microcentro; admission free; 🕐 10am-6pm Mon-Fri, 2-6pm Sun; Ⓜ Line A Plaza de Mayo, Line D Catedral, Line E Bolívar

Standing before this rosy Renaissance-style palace, you can easily imagine Eva Perón pontificating from the lower balcony. This is the Casa Rosada (Pink House), home to Argentina's presidential offices. Construction began in 1862 on the site of Buenos Aires' fort, and the building was painted pink shortly after. Visitors marvel at the picturesque coral hue without realizing the gritty fact behind it – at the end of the 19th century, ox blood added color and texture to ordinary whitewash.

📷 CATEDRAL METROPOLITANA

☎ 4331-2845; cnr Av Rivadavia & San Martín, Microcentro; admission free; 🕐 8am-7pm Mon-Fri, 9am-7:30pm Sat & Sun; Ⓜ Line A Perú, Line D Catedral, Line E Bolívar; ♿

A soaring baroque interior, an eye-catching rococo altar, an intricately tiled floor and a statue of Christ carved from the wood of an algarrobo (carob) tree distinguish the city's main cathedral. The mausoleum is the final resting place of the Liberator General José de San Martín, Argentina's independence leader, and an eternal flame burns outside in his honor.

CENTRO CULTURAL BORGES

☎ 5555-5359; www.ccborges.org.ar; Galerías Pacífico, cnr Viamonte & San Martín, Microcentro; admission $15; ☾ 10am-9pm Mon-Sat, noon-9pm Sun; Ⓜ Line C San Martín, Line C Lavalle; ♿

So, all right, it's in a shopping mall. But this cutting-edge cultural center, named for Argentina's literary giant, hosts major exhibits as well as smaller-scale shows by local artists. And, anyway, it's a really nice shopping mall – the upscale Galerías Pacífico (p40).

GALERÍA GÜEMES

Florida 165, Microcentro; ☾ 8:30am-5:30pm Ⓜ Line B Florida; ♿

The glittering Galería Güemes mall and theater

Here's a fun fact for die-hard fans of *The Little Prince*: Antoine de Saint-Exupéry once lived in an apartment here in the glittering Galería Güemes, now a shopping gallery and theater complex. The French pilot/writer met his wife, an El Salvadorean painter, at a demonstration in the streets of Buenos Aires, and *Night Flight* was based on his experience flying post in South America.

IGLESIA SANTA CATALINA

cnr Viamonte & San Martín, Microcentro; admission free; ☾ 8am-6pm, guided tours 3pm Fri; Ⓜ Line C Lavalle

Buenos Aires' first convent, Santa Catalina was founded in 1745 and later occupied by British troops during their second invasion in 1807. Look for the exquisite gilded fixtures and Baroque altarpiece by Spanish carver Isidro Lorea.

MANZANA DE LAS LUCES

☎ 4342-3964; www.manzanadelasluces .gov.ar, in Spanish; Perú 272, Microcentro; admission free, tours $5; ☾ noon-3pm Tue, Wed & Fri, 3-7pm Sat & Sun; Ⓜ Line A Plaza de Mayo, Line E Bolívar

The Manzana de las Luces (Block of Enlightenment) was once the meeting place of Argentina's intellectual heavyweights. The intriguing complex, connected to nearby buildings by a series of underground tunnels that were rediscovered in 1912, includes a university built by Jesuit missionaries in the early 1700s and the Iglesia de San Ignacio, BA's oldest church.

© MUSEO ETNOGRÁFICO

☎ 4331-7788; www.museoetnografico .filo.uba.ar; Moreno 350, Montserrat; admission $2; ⊙ 3-7pm Wed-Sun, closed Jan; Ⓜ Line A Plaza de Mayo, Line E Bolívar

Sad but true – indigenous groups inhabited the region before the arrival of European settlers. This petite museum pays tribute to the tribes, showing a collection of headdresses, ceramic bowls, decorative masks, cookware, religious relics and tools.

© OBELISCO

cnr Avs 9 de Julio & Corrientes, Congreso; Ⓜ Line B Carlos Pellegrini, Line D 9 de Julio

Inaugurated in 1936 on the 400th anniversary of the first Spanish settlement and stretching 68m skyward, El Obelisco is more than a point of orientation – love it or hate it, it's a striking symbol of modern Buenos Aires. The monument's popularity peaked in 2005 when it donned a huge pink condom for AIDS awareness day.

© PLAZA DE MAYO

cnr Avs de Mayo & Bolívar, Microcentro; Ⓜ Line A Plaza de Mayo; Line D Catedral, Line E Bolívar; ♿

Founded in 1580 as the city's first central plaza, Plaza de Mayo is the symbolic and physical center of Argentina's rocky history. The square's name commemorates the May Revolution (1810) that began Argentina's process of independence from Spain. Plaza de Mayo has seen it all – spirited crowds cheering as Evita shouted from the Casa Rosada's (p38) balcony, military bombings in 1955, the march of the Madres as they protest the 'disappearance' of their sons. See also p17.

🛍 SHOP

🛍 DARCOS TANGO
Souvenirs, Shoes

☎ 4326-0232; www.darcostango.com; Suipacha 259, Microcentro; ⊙ 10am-6pm Mon-Fri; Ⓜ Line C Diagonal Norte, Line D 9 de Julio

The tango shoes at Darcos aren't called 'magic shoes' for nothing – professional dancers swear by them. This charming little store is located near tango salon Confitería Ideal (p45), convenient if you're looking to trade in your flip-flops for something more glamorous before you hit the dance floor.

🛍 GALERÍAS PACÍFICO
Shopping Mall

☎ 5555-5110; www.galeriaspacifico .ar; cnr Florida & Av Córdoba, Microcentro; ⊙ 10am-10pm; Ⓜ Line C San Martín

STREET SMART

> Av 9 de Julio – A massive main boulevard, 16 lanes wide – you'll need several minutes just to cross from one side to the other.
> Av Alvear – Recoleta's posh boulevard, thick with ritzy boutiques and luxury hotels.
> Av Corrientes – The city's theater strip, a little Broadway lined with traditional pizzerias and high-brow bookstores.
> Av de Mayo – Grand, historic and architecturally stunning, this elegant avenue is BA's version of the Champs-Elysées.
> Av del Libertador – A busy artery in Recoleta running north–south along the river coast, lined by green parks and historic monuments.
> Av Santa Fe – A stylish but low-key shopping avenue running through Recoleta; also a major transportation route.
> Defensa – The picturesque cobblestoned main street of San Telmo, teeming with student bars, rustic *parrillas* and antique stores.
> Florida and Lavalle – The Microcentro's busy pedestrian thoroughfares. Quick lunch spots, inexpensive cinemas and touristy leather shops.

Built in 1889 by Paris department store Bon Marché, this elegant downtown shopping center contains mostly luxury designer brands. More impressive is the beautiful vaulted ceiling painted by five renowned Argentine artists, including Antonio Berni, and the Centro Cultural Borges (p39) upstairs.

☐ PLATA NATIVA
Jewelry, Handicrafts

☎ 4312-1398; www.platanativa.com; Florida 860, Microcentro; ⏱ 10am-6pm Mon-Fri; Ⓜ Line C Lavalle, Line C San Martín

Plata Nativa is owned and operated by a local trio with a passion for South American folk art. Traditional Mapuche Indian

designs inspired this collection of burnished silver candelabras, pendants and earrings made with large ruby-red jewels and ethnic oil paintings on fabric.

☐ PRÜNE
Leather, Fashion

☎ 4011-4300; www.prune.com.ar; Florida 481, Microcentro; ⏱ 10am-8pm; Ⓜ Line B Florida, Line C Lavalle

The Microcentro's pedestrian thoroughfares are jammed with leather shops and outlets, but Prüne's collection is easily the most sophisticated and contemporary. This downtown branch of the high-end line is one-stop shopping for distressed leather accessories from wide belts to shoulder bags.

☐ WINERY *Wine*

☎ 4343-7400; www.winery.com.ar, in Spanish; Diagonal Roque Saenz Peña 555; ⏱ 10am-10pm Mon-Fri, 11am-8pm Sat & Sun; Ⓜ Line D Catedral

Bottoms up – you can try before you buy at Winery. Pay for Argentine varietals by the glass, then snap up a bottle or two to take home.

🍴 EAT

🍴 BRASSERIE BERRY *French* $$

☎ 4394-5255; Tucumán 775, Microcentro; ⏱ 9am-7pm Mon-Wed, 9am-late Thu & Fri; Ⓜ Line C Lavalle

With its leather banquettes, classic French bistro chairs, blackboard wine lists and rich cuisine, this brasserie has an authentic Lyon feel. The place throngs with bankers and executives at lunch, then takes on a quieter, more romantic ambiance when the downtown crowd heads home for dinner.

🍴 CALIFORNIA BURRITO COMPANY (CBC) *Mexican* $

4328-3056; www.californiaburritoco .com, in Spanish; Lavalle 441, Microcentro; ⏱ noon-11pm Mon-Fri; Ⓜ Line B Florida; 🚌 93, 130, 152; ♿ Ⓥ 🚻

Craving guacamole? Pick up a burrito or a pair of soft-shell tacos at CBC, a budget-friendly Mexican fast-food joint opened in BA by American expats. The open-all-day taco bar is heaped high with fresh

California Burrito Company

toppings from beef and chicken to beans and hot *salsa verde*.

🍴 CASA ROCA *French* $$$

☎ 4393-5777; www.casa-roca.com.ar, in Spanish; San Martín 579, Microcentro; ⏱ 12:30-4pm Mon-Fri; Ⓜ Line B Florida; 🚌 93, 152

It's not every day that you can take a lunch break at a 19th-century Italian-Renaissance mansion. The onetime home of President General Roca is now an elegant restaurant only open for three-course meals at midday. You'll feel worlds (and centuries) away from the downtown clamor while dining on roasted chicken and *pommes frites*.

🍴 D'ORO *Italian* $$

☎ 4342-6959; www.doro-resto.com.ar; Perú 159, Microcentro; ⏱ 9am-12:30am Mon-Fri; 7pm-1am Sat; Ⓜ Line A Perú, Line E Bolívar; 🚌 22, 24

This tried-and-true Italian wine-bar turns out thin, crispy oven-baked pizzas, mushroom risotto, cappellini tossed with fresh basil and tomatoes, and garlic-topped focaccia bread. A friendly sommelier is on hand to recommend a glass of Cabernet, and atmosphere is busy and pleasantly casual – you'll have to squeeze in sideways at lunch.

PURA VIDA
Vegetarian, Organic $$
☎ 4393-0093; www.puravidabuenos aires.com; Reconquista 516, Microcentro; ☽ 9am-6pm Mon-Fri; Ⓜ Line B LN Alem; Ⓥ

Wheatgrass shots, anyone? This sleek and uber-healthy eatery helps counteract the effects of the high cholesterol porteño diet. Try the grilled chicken sandwich with mango and cilantro or the avocado citrus salad – you'll feel less guilty when you're indulging in a steak and a half-liter of Malbec later on.

TOMO 1
Modern Argentine $$$
☎ 4326-6695; www.tomo1.com.ar; Hotel Panamericano, Carlos Pellegrini 521, Microcentro; ☽ noon-3pm Mon-Fri & 7.30pm-1am Mon-Sat; Ⓜ Line B Carlos Pellegrini; ᐟ 10, 17, 29;

The decor may be fading, but foodies make a fuss over Tomo 1. Try the *prix fixe* menu and you'll understand why it's considered

one of the city's venerable haute-cuisine temples. Chef sisters Ada and Eve Concaro build the menu around seasonal produce, home-made pasta and fresh fish.

🍸 DRINK

🍸 CAFÉ RICHMOND *Cafe*
☎ 4322-1341; Florida 468, Microcentro; ☽ 7am-10pm Mon-Sat; Ⓜ Line B Florida, Line C Lavalle;

Another favorite of Jorge Luis Borges, the elegant old Café Richmond has been serving afternoon teas (and the great writer's favorite, hot chocolate) since 1917.

🍸 CAFÉ TORTONI *Cafe*
☎ 4342-4328; www.cafetortoni .com.ar, in Spanish; Av de Mayo 829, Microcentro; ☽ 7:30am-2am Mon-Sat, 9am-1am Sun; Ⓜ Line A Piedras, Line C Av de Mayo;

While tourists tend to outnumber locals at this landmark cafe (the oldest in the country), it still has a special place in the hearts of older porteños nostalgic for the good old days. Tango shows are held in a separate salon most nights at 9:30pm and 11pm.

🍸 LA CIGALE *Bar*
☎ 4312-8275; 25 de Mayo 722, Retiro; ☽ 6pm-late Mon-Fri, 8pm-late Sat; ᐟ 93, 130, 152

La Cigale's wide, curving bar, covered in twilight-blue tiles and

NEIGHBORHOODS

MICROCENTRO

A RIDE BACK IN TIME

Sentimental types who just can't get enough of Buenos Aires' old-fashioned charms can take a short journey into the city's past by boarding Subte (subway) line A in Plaza de Mayo. The quaint wooden train-cars are the originals from the system's construction in 1913. Ride west to the Castro Barros stop and the breathtaking **Las Violetas** (☎ 4958-7387; www.lasvioletas.com; cnr Rivadavia & Medrano), an antique cafe with gorgeous stained-glass windows, polished wood and a bakery turning out Parisian-style bonbons and pastries. The spectacular corner space opened in 1884. Ask for the sampler of exquisite little cakes and sandwiches, served with coffee and freshly squeezed orange juice.

attended by a handful of young cocktail-mixologists, forms the centerpiece of this artistic French-style bar. A few students and twentysomethings filter in early for happy-hour *mojito* specials, but you can barely fit in the door later when themed music nights pull a sizeable crowd.

▼ LA PUERTO RICO *Cafe*
☎ 4331-2215; www.lapuertoricocafe .com.ar, in Spanish; Adolfo Alsina 416, Montserrat; ☺ 7am-8pm Mon-Fri, 7am-4pm Sat; Ⓜ Line A Plaza de Mayo, Line E Bolívar; ♿ ☝
Cafe-hoppers with a sweet tooth shouldn't miss the freshly ground coffee and homemade chocolate

at the charming La Puerto Rico. Dating to 1887, the place features huge picture windows, pretty woodwork and a long zinc bar.

▼ LE BAR *Bar, Dance Club*
☎ 5219-0858; www.lebarbuenosaires .blogspot.com, in Spanish; Tucumán 422, Microcentro; ☺ noon-2am Mon-Sat; Ⓜ Line B Florida; 🚌 93, 152
Provocative design, in-demand DJs, splashy art and killer cocktails – Le Bar is the harbinger of downtown's nightlife Renaissance. The antique four-story building was redone to resemble a fanciful European parlor with tear-drop lamps casting a sexy glow across the jewel-toned interior. Come late to knock back the passion fruit–tinged *Pasiónaria* on the rooftop terrace or in futuristic dugout seating on the 2nd floor.

PLAY

☆ BAHREIN *Dance Club*
☎ 4315-2403; www.bahreinba.com; Lavalle 345, Microcentro; ☺ midnight-late Tue-Sat; Ⓜ Line B Florida, Line C Lavalle; ♿
Stained-glass windows and twinkling chandeliers don't usually work, design-wise, with seventies-style disco balls and modular sofas. But fabulous Bahrein has successfully retained the original fittings of the century-old building while drawing a thoroughly modern

late-night crowd to the 'Funky Room' disco, the electrónica party in the basement, and the laid-back Yellow Bar upstairs.

☆ BIG ONE *Dance Club*
☎ 4331-1277; Palacio Alsina, Adolfo Alsina 940, Microcentro; ⏲ 1.30am-late Fri & Sat; Ⓜ Line C Moreno, Line E Belgrano; �🚌 10, 17, 59, 64, 86
One night only, folks. On Saturdays, the wrought-iron Palacio Alsina is taken over by a parade of young revelers filing into Big One, the capital's biggest electrónica party. Internationally known DJs keep the sweaty festivities going all night with pumping house and techno; Friday nights (or, rather, Saturday mornings) see an equally huge gay party.

☆ COCOLICHE *Dance Club*
☎ 4331-6413; www.cocoliche.net; Av Rivadavia 878, Microcentro; ⏲ 11pm-late Tue-Sun; Ⓜ Line A Piedras; �🚌 10, 64, 100
This artistic underground club mixes a hipster crowd, and international DJs like Matthew Dear, with a first-class sound system. Show up in the middle of the night to see it at its most happening.

☆ CONFITERÍA IDEAL
Cafe, Tango
☎ 5265-8069; www.confiteriaideal .com; Suipacha 380, Microcentro;

⏲ 8am-late Tue-Sun; Ⓜ Line B Carlos Pellegrini, Line C Diagonal Norte, Line D 9 de Julio
Don't judge this downtown institution too quickly – the ground-level cafe is looking worn around the edges, but the upstairs dance hall, with its magnificent domed ceiling and glowing antique lanterns, is straight out of another era – especially when couples are locked together on the dance floor and old tango classics crackle over the loud speakers. See also p10.

☆ LUNA PARK *Concert Venue*
☎ 5279-5279; www.lunapark.com.ar, in Spanish; cnr Bouchard & Av Corrientes, Microcentro; Ⓜ Line B LN Alem
Luna Park is a historic performance venue: Juan Perón met his future wife, the young actress Eva Duarte, at a charity event here. Today this neon-signed classic hosts acts from the Harlem Globetrotters to Alanis Morissette.

☆ TEATRO GRAN REX
Concert Venue
☎ 4322-8000; Av Corrientes 857, Microcentro; Ⓜ Line B Carlos Pellegrini, Line C Diagonal Norte, Line D 9 de Julio
Everyone from Björk to Caetano Veloso has taken the stage at this classic theater and musical venue. Book a comfortable seat on the mezzanine level for the choicest view.

>PUERTO MADERO

Contemporary and squeaky clean, Puerto Madero isn't exactly bursting with local flavor – but it reveals a great deal about local aspirations. Porteños (BA locals) are fiercely proud of the dockside regeneration project that turned this old port into a prosperous commercial zone reminiscent of a London-style city harbor. The original Puerto Madero, located to the east of Plaza de Mayo, was the first sight glimpsed by European immigrants as they arrived in Buenos Aires. The port was abandoned after the turn of the century and left alone until ambitious developers kicked off a large-scale renovation of the area in the 1990s, cleaning up the dikes and ripping out rotting boards from the warehouses. Today, the red brick buildings house upscale restaurants, loft apartments and offices, a university and a handful of museums. The most impressive restoration effort was the brainchild of fashion-minded entrepreneur Alan Faena, who commissioned French designer Philippe Starck to help transform an old silo into the fabulous Faena Hotel + Universe in 2005. Further east, shaded bike paths traverse the expansive Reserva Ecológica Costanera Sur (ecological reserve). Take a siesta under the trees before strolling to Puerto Madero at sunset – the historic sailing vessels and ritzy party boats that bob in the water cut a striking silhouette against the flame-colored sunset.

PUERTO MADERO

☉ SEE
El Museo Fortabat 1 A2
Museo de la
 Inmigración 2 A1
Museo Fragata
 Sarmiento 3 A4
Puente de la Mujer 4 A3
Reserva Ecológica
 Costanera Sur 5 C3

🍴 EAT
Cabaña Las Lilas 6 A3
El Bistro 7 B4
i Fresh Market 8 A4
La Parolaccia
 del Mare 9 A4

🍸 DRINK
The Library Lounge 10 B4
White Bar 11 B5

★ PLAY
Asia de Cuba 12 A3
Puro Remo 13 A2

NEIGHBORHOODS

PUERTO MADERO

👁 SEE

👁 EL MUSEO FORTABAT

☎ 4310-6600; www.coleccionfortabat
.org.ar; Olga Cossettini 141, Puerto Madero Este; admission $15; ⏱ noon-9pm
Tue-Fri, 10am-9pm Sat & Sun; Ⓜ Line B
LN Alem; ♿

You have to hand it to an octoge-
narian who's also a millionaire, a
businesswoman, and the proud
owner of masterpieces by Andy
Warhol and Marc Chagall. This
sleek, newly opened dockside museum showcases the extraordinary
art collection of Amalia Lacroze de
Fortabat, including works by Salvador Dalí, Gustav Klimt, Auguste
Rodin and national visionaries like
Xul Solar and Clorindo Testa.

👁 MUSEO DE LA INMIGRACIÓN

☎ 4317-0285; Av Antártida Argentina
1355, Puerto Madero; admission by donation; ⏱ 10am-5pm Mon-Fri, 11am-6pm
Sat & Sun; 🚌 6, 20

At this engaging museum, old
photographs, films and artifacts
tell the stories of the European
immigrants who arrived in Buenos
Aires in the late 1880s.

👁 MUSEO FRAGATA SARMIENTO

☎ 4334-9386; Av Alicia Moreau de Justo
900, Dique 3, Puerto Madero; admission
$2; ⏱ 9am-8pm; Ⓜ Line B LN Alem

This elegant former naval ship
has a storied past – it sailed
around the world 40 times
between 1899 and 1938 before
serving as a training school for
Argentina's navy. Hop aboard to
check out the antique nautical
gadgets.

👁 PUENTE DE LA MUJER

Dique 3, Puerto Madero; Ⓜ Line B LN
Alem; ♿

Puerto Madero is femme-friendly:
all the streets in the neighborhood are named after famous
ladies, and the striking Puente de
la Mujer (Bridge of the Woman) is
the barrio's signature monument.
Unveiled in 2001, the stunningly

ROW YOUR BOAT ASHORE

Due to water pollution near the city
center, most of the aquatic activity on
the Rio de la Plata occurs in the coastal
northern suburbs. But a couple of kayak
outfitters are attempting to bring some
recreation back to the urban waters.
Stroll down to **Puro Remo** (☎ 6397-
3545; www.puroremo.com.ar, in Spanish; cnr Juana Manso & Victoria Ocampo)
at Puerto Madero's Yacht Club to look
into your paddling and rowing options.
Offering kayak rental, guided tours and
clean, efficient facilities, the business
also runs longer trips including *asados*
(barbecues) and island excursions in the
Tigre river delta.

Stroll across the Puente de la Mujer

contemporary gleaming-white structure was designed by acclaimed Spanish architect Santiago Calatreva and represents – what else? – a couple dancing the tango.

RESERVA ECOLÓGICA COSTANERA SUR *Park*
☎ 4893-1588; Av Tristán Achaval Rodríguez 1550, Puerto Madero; ☽ 8am-6pm Tue-Sun Apr-Sep, 8am-7pm Oct-Mar; 🚌 2, 130, 152; ♿ ☗
Birdwatchers and cyclists find an urban haven in the lovely Reserva Ecológica, a sprawling green space bordered on one side by the Río de la Plata and on the other by the Costanera Sur promenade.

🍴 EAT
🍴 CABAÑA LAS LILAS
Parrilla $$$
☎ 4313-1336; www.laslilas.com, in Spanish; Av Alicia Moreau de Justo 516, Dique 4, Puerto Madero; ☽ noon-4pm & 7.30pm-1am; Ⓜ Line B LN Alem; ♿ ☗
Porteños are evenly split as to whether this famous eatery is a fantastically overpriced display of hubris or an upmarket example of *parrilla* perfection. Tellingly, even those who deride this large waterside restaurant won't hesitate to thumb through the jumbo wine list, especially if the meal's on someone else's dime. The fine beef was raised on the restaurant's own *estancia* (ranch).

ⅥⅠ EL BISTRO *International* $$$

☎ 4010-9200; www.faenahoteland
universe.com; Faena Hotel + Universe,
Martha Salotti 445, Dique 2, Puerto
Madero; ⏱ 8pm-1am; Ⓜ Line B LN
Alem; 🚌 2, 130, 152; ♿

Don't despair if you're not
staying at the otherworldly
Philippe Starck–designed Faena
Hotel + Universe (complete with
'personal experience managers,'
a gentlemen's club–style bar, a
cabaret theater and a luxe pool
bar). You can still spend a stack of
pesos at El Bistro. Design geeks
and foodies alike are entranced by
this blindingly white space punc-
tuated with blood-red accents and
whimsical plaster unicorns. The
flamboyant decor nearly distracts
dinner guests from the exquisite
degustación (tasting) menus
prepared by award-winning chef
Mariano Cid de la Paz.

ⅥⅠ I FRESH MARKET
Deli, Cafe $$

☎ 5775-0335; cnr Azucena Villaflor &
Olga Cossettini, Dique 3, Puerto Madero;
⏱ 8am-late; 🚌 2, 130, 152; ♿ Ⓥ ♿

This chic deli-cafe-restaurant
feels like it belongs in Manhattan,
serving espresso and pastries in
the morning and fresh vegetable
wraps for lunch. The gourmet
marketplace inside will tempt
you to blow all your cash on rich
chocolates and cheeses. For a

Get back to nature at the Reserva Ecolólogica Costanera Sur (p49)

sophisticated dinner by the water, head to the deli's sister restaurant, i Central Market, on the corner of Dealessi and Güemes.

🍴 LA PAROLACCIA DEL MARE
Italian $$

☎ 4343-1679; www.laparolaccia.com; Av Alicia Moreau de Justo 1052, Dique 3, Puerto Madero; 🕑 noon-midnight; Ⓜ Line B LN Alem; Ⓥ

The classy Italian restaurant La Parolaccia has a few locations scattered throughout BA's ritzier barrios; this particular branch specializes in seafood. Reserve a table along the waterfront windows and savor tasty pasta or risotto tossed with freshly caught *mariscos* (shellfish).

DRINK
🍸 THE LIBRARY LOUNGE *Bar*

☎ 4010-9200; www.faenahoteland universe.com; Faena Hotel + Universe, Martha Salotti 445, Dique 2, Puerto Madero; 🕑 9am-2pm; Ⓜ Line B LN Alem; 🚍 2, 130, 152; ♿

The low-lit Library Lounge, all dark wood with plush forest-green armchairs and stuffed moose-heads, feels out of another era. It's the kind of place where gentlemen once gathered to smoke

cigars, play billiards and schmooze. Order a classic martini and let the sultry lounge singer do her thing. Rojo Tango, the sexy cabaret dinner show staged at the adjacent theater, is great, decadent fun – be sure to book ahead.

🍸 WHITE BAR *Bar*

☎ 5776-7677; www.hotelmadero.com; Hotel Madero, Rosario Vera Peñaloza 360, Dique 2; 🕑 7-10:30am, noon-4pm, 7pm-1am; 🚍 2, 130, 152

Lobby bars at five-star hotels often lack character, but the fashionable Hotel Madero, with a long white bar with funky white plastic stools, is an ideal drop-in spot for a pre-dinner cocktail.

PLAY
⭐ ASIA DE CUBA *Bar, Club*

☎ 4894-1328; www.asiadecuba.com.ar, in Spanish; Dealessi 750, Puerto Madero Este; 🕑 9pm-late Tue-Sat; 🚍 2, 130, 152

This Asian-style lounge bar and club has lost some of its luster in recent years, but the exotic Shanghai-inspired decor and eclectic dance music still bring in well-dressed locals and party-going tourists. The gorgeous cushioned outdoor seating, facing the water, is delightful.

>CONGRESO & TRIBUNALES

Unlike the various barrios catering to the tourist dollar, Congreso and Tribunales hold fiercely to their stately Spanish roots – the art-nouveau structures along Av de Mayo may be crumbling in places, but they're still there, and traditional cafes still outnumber trendy cocktail bars. This is the 'other' downtown, separated from the Microcentro by Av 9 de Julio. Cross the 16 lanes of speeding traffic to enter this old-fashioned, slightly gritty world where rich and poor often live on the same block. Picturesque Av de Mayo runs through the heart of the barrio and features most of Congreso's historical sites. A compelling range of architectural styles – from enormous belle-epoque edifices around Plaza del Congreso to the neocolonial apartment buildings of Montserrat – make the barrio a fascinating place to wander on a sunny afternoon. The neighborhood is far from being a hot spot for dining and drinking, but traditional Spanish restaurants and cafes proliferate as you walk north through Tribunales toward bustling Av Corrientes, the center of the theater district and home to dozens of pizzerias, cinemas and bookshops. The barrio's crowning glory is the city's grand dame of an opera house, the spectacular Teatro Colón.

CONGRESO & TRIBUNALES

⊙ SEE
El Molino 1 B4
Palacio Barolo 2 C4
Palacio de las Aguas
    Corrientes 3 A2
Palacio del Congreso 4 B4
Plaza del Congreso 5 C4

⌂ SHOP
Arte de Pueblos 6 D1
Club de Tango 7 C3
Gandhi Galerna 8 B3

⍟ EAT
El Cuartito 9 C1
Plaza Asturias 10 D4
Restó 11 C1
Status 12 C4

☲ DRINK
Bar Iberia 13 D4
Café Literario Osvaldo
    Bayer 14 C4
Cruzat Beer House 15 C3
El Living 16 C1

★ PLAY
36 Billares 17 D4
El Beso 18 B3
Maluco Beleza 19 B3
Teatro Colón 20 D2
Teatro Nacional
    Cervantes 21 D1
Teatro San Martín 22 C3

SEE

EL MOLINO

Av Callao 10, Congreso; M Line A Congreso

This broke-down beauty, reminiscent of Paris' Moulin Rouge, was once an elegant cafe where politicians socialized between meetings at Palacio del Congreso. Sadly, the striking art-nouveau corner building is now covered in cobwebs after closing in 1996. Conservation teams struggle to raise funds to restore El Molino (the Windmill), still considered an architectural landmark.

PALACIO BAROLO

☎ 4383-1065; www.pbarolo.com.ar; Av de Mayo 1370, Congreso; M Line A Sáenz Peña, Line B Uruguay

In 1919, Italian cotton tycoon Luis Barolo commissioned architect Mario Palanti to build a tribute to Dante's *Divine Comedy*. The stunning neo-Gothic Palacio Barolo rises 100m and 22 floors – symbolizing the masterpiece's 100 songs, composed of 22 verses each – and the floors of the ground level ('Hell') are inlaid with flame-like designs. The next 14 floors, now office space, represent 'Purgatory,' while the uppermost floors and tower, offering spectacular views over the city, are 'Paradise.'

PALACIO DE LAS AGUAS CORRIENTES

☎ 6319-1104; Riobamba 750, Congreso; ☼ 9am-1pm Mon-Fri, closed Jan & Feb; M Line D Callao or Facultad de Medicina

Hundreds of thousands of glazed terracotta tiles adorn the exterior of this awe-inspiring building. Opened in 1894, the fairytale-like Palacio de Las Aguas Corrientes (Palace of Running Water) was home to 12 giant tanks that distributed water to the city. Now the building has a small museum exhibiting antique faucets and urinals.

PALACIO DEL CONGRESO

☎ 4010-3000; cnr Avs Entre Ríos & Rivadavia, Congreso; M Line A Congreso; ♿

The colossal greystone Palacio del Congreso, Argentina's national House of Congress, was structurally inspired by the Capitol in Washington, DC. Completed in 1906, it's topped by an enormous 85m dome and splendid statuary.

PLAZA DEL CONGRESO

Av de Mayo, Congreso; M Line A Congreso; ♿

Plaza del Congreso sees a daily parade of children sprinting toward the carousel, and dog walkers trying to keep up with

Palacio Barolo watching over Avenida de Mayo

GARDEL & THE TANGO

In June 1935 a woman committed suicide in Havana, and a woman in New York and another in Puerto Rico tried to poison themselves, all over the same man – whom none of them had ever met. This man was tango singer Carlos Gardel, El Zorzal Criollo, the songbird of Buenos Aires, who had just died in a plane crash in Colombia.

Though born in France (or perhaps Uruguay, it's disputed), Gardel was the epitome of the immigrant porteño (BA local). In his youth, he worked at a variety of menial jobs and entertained his neighbors with his rapturous singing. He first performed with Uruguayan-born José Razzano, before collaborating with lyricist Alfredo Le Pera and creating several tango classics such as *Por Una Cabeza*. His beautiful baritone voice, matinee-idol looks and charisma made him a success in Latin America, and later in Paris and New York, during the 1920s and 1930s. His promising career as a Paramount movie star was cut short by the air crash in which his collaborator, Le Pera, was also killed.

A steady procession of pilgrims still visits Carlos Gardel's home (now a museum; see p108) and his sarcophagus in the Cementerio de la Chacarita in Buenos Aires, where a lit cigarette often smolders between the metal fingers of his life-size statue and, as the saying goes, 'Gardel sings better every day.'

their charges. Permanent fixtures include the Monumento a los Dos Congresos, which, with high steps symbolizing the Andes and a fountain representing the Atlantic Ocean, honors the congresses that led Argentina to independence.

 SHOP

ARTE DE PUEBLOS
Souvenirs, Handicrafts

☎ 4816-4351; www.artedepueblos.org
.ar, in Spanish; Libertad 948, Tribunales;
🕙 10am-7:30pm Mon-Fri, 10am-1pm
Sat; Ⓜ Line D Tribunales
Shop with a clear conscience at Arte de Pueblos. Fair-trade crafts produced by indigenous artisans

in the Argentine provinces of Salta, Formosa, and Río Negro use natural materials and traditional techniques to produce this range of wooden utensils, woven belts, ceramic bowls and ethnic jewelry.

CLUB DE TANGO
Souvenirs

☎ 4372-7251; www.clubdetango.com
.ar, in Spanish; office 114, 5th flr, Paraná
123, Congreso; 🕙 11am-6pm Mon-Fri;
Ⓜ Line B Uruguay
Snap up tango souvenirs at this wonderful shop stocked with memorabilia such as Carlos Gardel posters and photo books, and tango lessons on DVD.

GANDHI GALERNA
Bookstore

☎ 4374-7574; www.galernalibros
.com, in Spanish; Av Corrientes 1743,
Microcentro; ⏱ 10am-10pm Mon-Thu,
10am- midnight Fri & Sat, 4-10pm Sun;
Ⓜ Line B Callao; ♿

If you wear black and keep your
mouth shut you might pass for
one of the local intellectuals,
academics, artists and writers who
make this bookshop their second
home. Among the philosophy
and literature volumes, you'll find
tango books and a diverse selection of Latin American music, from
rock nacional (Argentine rock) to
Brazilian samba.

EAT

EL CUARTITO
Italian, Argentine $

☎ 4816-1758; Talcahuano 937, Tribunales; ⏱ noon-late; Ⓜ Line D Tribunales;
🚌 152, 111; Ⓥ

Since 1934, this legendary pizzeria
has seen local men polishing off
slices at the counter and families
sharing fresh *empanadas* (savory-
filled pastries) at tables, surrounded by faded images of sportsmen.

PLAZA ASTURIAS
Spanish, Seafood $$$

☎ 4382-7334; Cnr Av de Mayo & Salta,
Congreso; ⏱ noon-late; Ⓜ Line A Lima;
♿ 🚹

The dated decor at Plaza Asturias
assures you that this is no cutting-
edge Spanish eatery – no foams,
mousses or organic produce here,
just heaping portions of shrimp,
mussels and clams tossed with
garlic and herbs. Try the pungent
cazuela de mariscos (seafood stew;
a flavorful antidote to the meat-
heavy cuisine at other restaurants)
that will jolt your palate and clear
up your sinuses.

RESTÓ
Modern Argentine, French $$

☎ 4816-6711; Montevideo 938, Tribunales; ⏱ noon-3pm Mon-Fri, 8-11pm
Thu & Fri; Ⓜ Line D Callao

María Barrutia's painstakingly
artistic presentations of quail and
salmon contrast sharply with her
restaurant's understated environs.
The illustrious chef whips up slow
food that is either a smash hit – a
rich, creamy pumpkin soup – or a
flop. Either way, she's experimental, and she makes a splash on the
local dining scene. Try her creative
daily menu at Restó.

STATUS *Peruvian* $

☎ 4382-8531; Virrey Cevallos 178,
Congreso; ⏱ noon-5pm & 8pm-1am
Mon-Thu, noon-1am Fri-Sun; Ⓜ Line A
Sáenz Peña; Ⓥ 🚹

Raw shark and a purple corn
cocktail? It tastes much better
than it sounds, Status' devotees

will guarantee you. This no-frills eatery, packing in a nightly crowd with roasted chicken and rice, fresh shark *ceviche* (lemon-marinated fish), creamy potatoes and cinnamon-topped pisco sours, is a gastronomic standout in a part of town that's rife with traditional Peruvian restaurants.

DRINK

☷ BAR IBERIA *Cafe, Bar*
☎ 4381-6300; cnr Av de Mayo & Salta, Congreso; ☽ 24hr; Ⓜ Line A Lima; ♿ ♨

Soak up the grandeur of Av de Mayo at Bar Iberia, the city's second-oldest cafe. Since 1897, the sophisticated corner bar has welcomed distinguished clientele like playwright Federico García Lorca, who lived for a time at the nearby Castelar Hotel. Take in the avenue's magnificent architecture from the sidewalk table.

☷ CAFÉ LITERARIO OSVALDO BAYER *Cafe*
☎ 4382-3261; Hipólito Yrigoyen 1584, Congreso; ☽ noon-9pm; Ⓜ Line A Congreso, Line A Sáenz Peña

The Madres de la Plaza de Mayo run this small cafe and eatery, in conjunction with their bookstore at their headquarters – a hub of liberal politics where students scan the papers to see if any children of the *desaparecidos* (disappeared ones) have been located. The cafe is modest, but the atmosphere is unique. See also p17.

☷ CRUZAT BEER HOUSE *Bar*
☎ 6320-5344; www.cruzatba.com; Sarmiento 1617, Congreso; ☽ 10am-2am Mon-Sat, 5pm-2am Sun; Ⓜ Line B Callao

---

WORTH THE TRIP

Located way out in the western suburbs, the lighthearted folk festival **Feria de Mataderos** (☎ 4687-5602; www.feriademataderos.com.ar, in Spanish; cnr Avs Lisandro de la Torre & de los Corrales; ☽ 1-9pm Sun & holidays Apr-Nov, 6pm-midnight Sat Dec-Mar) will take almost an hour to reach by bus 155 or 126 – but the journey's worth it. Brilliantly costumed teenagers perform folkloric dances on stage while gauchos on horseback compete in traditional contests and local ladies dish out hearty country-style food and sweet *patero* wine. Over 100 craft stalls sell affordable handmade treasures from horse-hoof ashtrays to leather and metalwork; indulge yourself along the strip of gourmet food stalls where vendors offer free samples of *dulce de leche* liqueur, cheeses, and homemade liquors. For details on upcoming festivals, check their website. The long bus ride to Mataderos is a cultural experience in itself – but travelers on a strict schedule can also arrive by taxi.

NEIGHBORHOODS

CONGRESO & TRIBUNALES

Choose a beer or five from the enormous menu at Cruzat Beer House

In wine-soaked Buenos Aires, Cruzat is as close as you can get to a German beer garden. Kick back on the shaded terrace and choose from a thick menu of over 150 microbrews – or ask for the beer tasting. A selection of a dozen draught beers, served in miniature glasses, will come right to your table.

☒ EL LIVING Bar, Club

☎ 4811-4730; www.living.com.ar, in Spanish; Marcelo T de Alvear 1540, Retiro; ☽ 10pm-late Thu-Sat; ☒ 10, 39, 102, 152 Laid-back El Living (the Living Room) sticks to a decade-old formula: plush sofas, cheap whiskey sours, campy George Michael

music videos projected onto a huge screen, and a young, cheerful crowd. Before 2am, dinner guests linger and most bar stools are empty, but you'll be squished between vintage Madonna fans when the '80s dance party gets going in the wee hours.

☆ PLAY

☆ 36 BILLARES Billiards, Tango

☎ 4381-5696; www.los36billares.com .ar; Av de Mayo 1265, Congreso; ☽ 8am-2am; Ⓜ Line A Lima Shoot pool with some elderly gents – or just catch a performance by a sultry singer in the main cafe – at this antique bar where the

Argentine Billiards Association was born in 1926. The nightly tango show verges on the burlesque.

⭐ EL BESO *Tango*

☎ 4953-2794; Riobamba 416, Tribunales; 🕙 from 9pm Tue, 10.30pm Wed, 6pm Thu, 11pm Sat & 10pm Sun; Ⓜ Line B Callao

This traditional tango salon brings in some 2000 *tangueros* (traditional tango dancers) every week for its dynamic *milongas* (social dances) and daily classes. Despite the increased presence of curious tourists, El Beso maintains a wonderfully authentic atmosphere.

⭐ MALUCO BELEZA
Dance Club

☎ 4372-1737; www.malucobeleza .com.ar, in Spanish; Sarmiento 1728, Tribunales; 🕙 1am-late Wed & Fri-Sun; Ⓜ Line B Callao

This energetic Brazilian club is the place to go when you're experiencing tango overload. If samba's not your thing, there's house music upstairs.

⭐ TEATRO COLÓN
Theater

☎ 4378-7344; Libertad 621, Tribunales, tours depart from Tucumán 1171; 🕙 performance times vary; Ⓜ Line D Tribunales; 🚌 23, 29, 39, 75, 99, 102, 115, 140; ♿ 🚻

Sinking into a red velvet seat for a performance at Teatro Colón is undeniably one of Buenos Aires' most magical experiences – too bad the place has been closed for renovations for over two years. The whole of BA eagerly awaits the re-opening of one of the world's great opera houses, which was opened in 1908 and called by Mikhail Baryshnikov 'the most beautiful of the theaters I know.'

CONTEMPORARY GALLERIES

Intrigued by Buenos Aires' edgy art scene? Stop by one of the major galleries to behold creative works from photography to sculpture – or, better yet, show up at an exhibition opening to sip champagne and check out the art folk in action. On the north side of the city, **Braga Menendez Arte Contemporaneo** (Map pp114–15, C3; ☎ 4775-5577; www .galeriabm.com; Humboldt 1574, Villa Crespo; 🕙 1-8pm Mon-Fri & 2-6pm Sat-Sun; closed Jan-Feb) shows contemporary work by dozens of independent artists. Downtown, swing by a tried-and-true art institution, **Ruth Benzacar** (Map p63, C3; ☎ 4313-8480; www .ruthbenzacar.com; Florida 1000, Retiro; 🕙 11:30am-8pm Mon-Fri), or continue south to San Telmo's stylish new **Zavaleta Lab** (Map p71, B2; ☎ 5290-4640; www.zavaletalab.com; Venezuela 567, San Telmo; 🕙 11am-8pm Mon-Fri & 11am-2pm Sat).

WORTH THE TRIP

The venue is off the beaten path, but true tango enthusiasts shouldn't forgo a trip to El Niño Bien, one of the city's most atmospheric *milongas*. Held on Thursday nights at the **Centro Region Leonesa** (☎ 4147-8867; Humberto Primo 1462; admission $20; 🕑 8pm-late Mon, 6pm-late Wed, Fri & Sat, 10:30pm-late Thu & Sat; 🚌 39, 60, 102), the event sees porteño couples embracing and twirling dramatically around a spectacular wooden dance floor as strains of Carlos Gardel's 'Mi Noche Triste' (My Sad Night) crackle through the antique sound system. El Niño Bien is charmingly local – in other words, not designed for tourists – so if you're just going to observe the scene, don't blind the dancers with your camera flash. Just grab a table for two and play it cool with a bottle of Cabernet. Consider booking ahead, as the regular *tangueros* are quick to snap up the tables skirting the dance floor. If you're not in town on a Thursday, catch the afternoon *milonga* here on Wednesdays and Fridays, or swing by after dinner – the building hosts low-key *milongas* most nights of the week.

⭐ **TEATRO NACIONAL CERVANTES** *Theater*
☎ 4816-4224; www.teatrocervantes .gov.ar, in Spanish; Libertad 815, Tribu- nales; 🕑 box office 10am-8pm, closed Jan; Ⓜ Line D Tribunales; ♿ 🚻
This architectural gem, featuring an ornate lobby and sumptuous velvet seats, is a classic venue to catch musicals and dance performances.

⭐ **TEATRO SAN MARTÍN** *Theater*
☎ 0800-333-5254; Av Corrientes 1530, Tribunales; 🕑 performance times vary; Ⓜ Line B Uruguay; 🚌 24, 60, 102; ♿ 🚻
This 1970's-style theater may lack old-fashioned charm, but the diverse agenda of Spanish ballet, children's musicals, French plays, classic films and alternative theater makes San Martín a staple of the Corrientes strip.

>RETIRO

In Spanish, Retiro means 'retreat,' which refers to the country villa and surrounding gardens that Spanish politician Agustín de Robles established here in the late 17th century. Lovely Plaza San Martín, with its twisting *palo rosa* trees and sloping green lawn, still conjures up images of the original estate – but yesterday's aristocracy would be shocked to see that today's Retiro also contains one of the city's largest *villas* (shantytowns). Apart from the poverty-stricken encampment that sprawls northward from the central train station, the barrio is stylish and upscale, boasting several ritzy hotels and palaces, architectural landmarks like the Edificio Kavanagh and the Torre de los Ingleses, and a number of fashionable bistros and bars that line San Martín and its parallel street Reconquista. Fans of writer Jorge Luis Borges can take a look at his modest apartment building at Maipú 994.

RETIRO

🔵 SEE
Edificio Kavanagh 1 C3
Museo Municipal de Arte
 Hispanoamericano Isaac
 Fernández Blanco 2 B2
Plaza San Martín 3 C3
Torre de los Ingleses 4 D2

🏠 SHOP
Autoría 5 B3
Casa Lopez 6 C3

El Remanso 7 C3
JCB Gems & Carvings 8 C3
Ligier 9 C3
Tierra Adentro 10 B2

🍴 EAT
El Establo 11 D3
Empire Thai 12 D4
Filo 13 D3
Irifune 14 D4
Le Sud 15 C2
Sipan 16 C4

🍸 DRINK
Café Retiro 17 C2
Dadá 18 D3
Marriott Plaza Bar 19 C3

⭐ PLAY
ND/Ateneo 20 B4

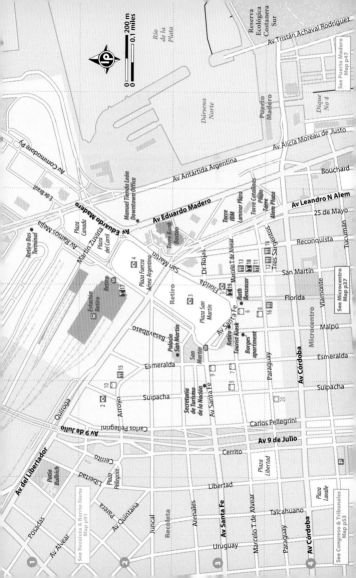

200 m
0.1 miles

Río de la Plata

Reserva Ecológica Costanera Sur

Av Tristán Achaval Rodríguez

Dársena Norte

Dique No 4

See Puerto Madero Map p47

Puerto Madero

Av Alicia Moreau de Justo

Av Commodore Py

E de Basi

Av Antártida Argentina

Av Eduardo Madero

Bouchard

Manuel Tienda León Downtown Office

Av Ramos Mejía

Retiro Bus Terminal

Plaza Canadá

Martín Zuvíria Plaza del Carril

Av Eduardo Madero

Av Leandro N Alem

25 de Mayo

Torre Bank Boston

Reconquista

Tucumán

Torre IBM

Laminar Plaza

Torre Catalinas

Pilar Torre Alem Plaza

San Martín

Tres Sargentos

Plaza Fuerza Aérea Argentina

4

Retiro

San Martín

Dr Rojas

Florida

Marcelo T de Alvear

12 🍴 19
13
18 🍴
11

See Microcentro Map p37

Estación Retiro

17 🍴

3

Plaza San Martín

19 🍴

Ruth Benzacar

San Martín

Florida

Viamonte

Basavilbaso

Palacio San Martín

Retiro Santa Fe
Tourist Kiosk

Av Santa Fe

6

8 🍴

16 🍴

Microcentro

Maipú

San Martín

Borges apartment

Paraguay

Esmeralda

Esmeralda

15 🍴

10

2 🛏

Arroyo

Suipacha

Secretaría de Turismo de la Nación

Av Santa Fe

9

5 🛏

7

Suipacha

Av Córdoba

Quiroga

Av 9 de Julio

Carlos Pellegrini

Av 9 de Julio

20 🍴

Cerrito

Cerrito

Av del Libertador

Patio Bullrich

Libertad

Plaza Pellegrini

Libertad

Plaza Libertad

Av Santa Fe

Marcelo T de Alvear

Plaza Lavalle

Av Córdoba

See Recoleta & Barrio Norte Map p91

Posadas

Av Alvear

Av Quintana

Parera

Juncal

Recoleta

Arenales

Uruguay

Paraguay

Talcahuano

See Congreso & Tribunales Map p53

1

2

3

4

SEE

EDIFICIO KAVANAGH
Florida 1035, Retiro; Ⓜ Line C San Martín
A feisty Irishwoman funded the construction of this handsome 120m art-deco apartment building, which was the tallest skyscraper in Latin America at the time of its construction in 1935. A local rumor claims that the heiress, vengeful towards another aristocratic family for scorning her daughter, built the structure that high to block light from entering the basilica where her rivals attended Mass every Sunday.

MUSEO MUNICIPAL DE ARTE HISPANOAMERICANO ISAAC FERNÁNDEZ BLANCO
☎ 4327-0228; Suipacha 1422; admission $3, free on Thu; ⏱ 2-7pm Tue-Sun; 🚌 93, 130, 152
Situated in a Peruvian-inspired baroque mansion, this museum displays Latin American colonial art including Jesuit statuary, engravings, textiles, silver and antiques. Chamber orchestra performances enliven the lovely Spanish-style gardens during the warmer months (October to April).

PLAZA SAN MARTÍN
Av Santa Fe & Florida, Retiro; Ⓜ Line C San Martín; ♿
Carlos Thays designed Plaza San Martín, the center's prettiest green space, on a gently sloping bluff. The park benches fill quickly on warm afternoons with sandwich-toting accountants and amorous couples. The imposing bronze and marble monument honors the South American liberator San Martín.

TORRE DE LOS INGLESES
Plaza Fuerza Aérea Argentina, Retiro; Ⓜ Line C San Martín
Big Ben in Buenos Aires. This 76m clock tower, located just across Plaza San Martín (left), was donated by the city's British community in 1910. Decades later, it was a bomb target during the 1982 Falklands War.

SHOP

AUTORÍA
Art, Home Decor
☎ 5252-2474; www.autoriabsas.com.ar, in Spanish; Suipacha 1025, Retiro; ⏱ 9:30am-8pm Mon-Fri, 10am-2pm & 4:30-8pm Sat; Ⓜ Line C San Martín
This cool designers' showcase, stocked with make-a-statement silver jewelry, edgy art books and whimsical leather desk sculptures, brings a welcome taste of the avant-garde to this suit-and-tie neighborhood.

Ricardo Liniers
Comic Artist and Painter

Are newspaper comics an art form in Buenos Aires? Yes, the form has a rich history. Excellent artwork has long been present in our everyday culture. **Describe your porteño audience.** This is a psychoanalyzed city. People talk about how pretentious or chauvinistic porteños can be. But we are warm, too, open to new people and ideas. **What about the traditional art scene?** I'm inspired by the younger artists like Germán Wendel and Nahuel Vecino [past exhibits at Centro Cultural Recoleta (p93) and Centro Cultural Borges (p39)] and Daniel Santoro, who plays with Peronist themes. Every time I save enough cash to buy a new refrigerator, I accidentally buy a painting instead. **Where do you live and work?** Retiro. **Best place to go for drinks?** Ølsen (p121.) **For dinner?** Sudestada (p122) – the food is so hot. I love when it's difficult, like a little job, to eat your food.

CASA LOPEZ *Leather*

☎ 4311-3044; www.casalopez.com.ar; Marcelo T de Alvear 640/658, Retiro; ⏰ 9am-8pm Mon-Fri, 9:30am-7pm Sat, 10am-6pm Sun; Ⓜ Line C San Martín

For boots and briefcases that'll last a lifetime, head to Casa Lopez, a shop that's been selling high-quality leather jackets, luggage, bags and accessories since 1943. Go elsewhere for youthful fashion – the style here is conservative and classic.

EL REMANSO *Leather*

☎ 4312-1879; Esmeralda 1018, Retiro; ⏰ 9am-7pm Mon-Fri, 10am-5pm Sat; Ⓜ Line C San Martín

The city's suavest gentlemen – polo players, obviously – roll up to outfitters like this one for dapper leather boots and stylish riding gear fit for their chiseled physiques. See the thoroughbreds in action at the polo grounds in Las Cañitas (p133).

JCB GEMS & CARVINGS
Jewelry, Souvenirs

☎ 4312-7517; Paraguay 627; ⏰ 10am-8pm Mon-Fri, 10am-4pm Sat; Ⓜ Line C San Martín

Woo your sweetheart (or treat yourself) with the romantic petal-pink *rodocrosita*, Argentina's unofficial national stone. This family-run gem and mineral shop carries artisan-produced pieces from gemstone earrings to handcrafted silver bracelets.

LIGIER *Wine, Gourmet Deli*

☎ 4515-0126; www.ligier.com.ar, in Spanish; cnr Av Santa Fe & Esmeralda, Retiro; ⏰ 9:30am-8pm Mon-Fri, 10am-2pm & 4-8pm Sat; Ⓜ Line C San Martín; ♿

This upmarket *vinoteca* and gourmet food chain deals primarily with tourists, which explains cheesy packages like the Teatro Colón wine collection. Nonetheless, Ligier is a foolproof stop when you need to pick up last-minute gifts (or a bottle of bubbly to take back to the hotel room).

TIERRA ADENTRO
Souvenirs, Handicrafts

☎ 4393-8552; Arroyo 882, Retiro; ⏰ 10am-8pm Mon-Fri, 10am-6pm Sat; 🚌 93, 130, 152

Tierra Adentro works with nonprofit organizations to help preserve indigenous communities in northern Argentina. Fair-trade practices brought this fine range of hand-woven cushion covers, colorful wall hangings and striking Mapuche silver necklaces to the capital city.

🍴 EAT

🍴 EL ESTABLO *Parrilla* $$

☎ 4311-1639; Paraguay 489, Retiro; ⏰ 7am-2am; Ⓜ Line C San Martín; ♿ 🚻

While it gets its fair share of tourists, trusty old El Establo is unlikely to have a tango show or wi-fi anytime soon. Try the Spanish tapas paired with the house red, then turn your attention to the true star of the show, the skillful *parrillero* (grill man).

EMPIRE THAI *Thai* $$$

☎ 4312-5706; www.empirethai.net; Tres Sargentos 427, Retiro; ⏰ noon-1am Mon-Fri, 7pm-2am Sat; 🚌 93, 152; ♿ Ⓥ

The sultry lighting and sumptuous decor are your first clue that this place isn't a traditional ethnic diner; the second is when you're still hungry after finishing your noodles. Never mind – the scrumptious peanut satay and the moody New York ambiance draw a cool crowd, and flavors like coconut and lemongrass give your palate a rest from all the steak you've probably consumed elsewhere.

FILO *Italian* $$

☎ 4311-0312; www.filo-ristorante .com, in Spanish; San Martín 975, Retiro; ⏰ noon-midnight; Ⓜ Line C San Martín; ♿ Ⓥ 👶

Popular with the 45-minutes-and-gone business lunch crowd and, by night, couples out on their third dinner date, this large, pop-art-style Italian pizzeria tosses thin-crust pies with fresh toppings. Try one piled high with prosciutto and arugula, then throw back some limoncello before checking out the downstairs art gallery.

IRIFUNE *Japanese* $$$

☎ 4312-8787; Paraguay 436, Retiro; ⏰ noon-3pm & 8pm-midnight Mon-Sat; 🚌 10, 93, 152; Ⓥ

Irifune quietly serves traditional Japanese in a minimalist setting. The service isn't rushed and the sushi isn't cheap – this is a

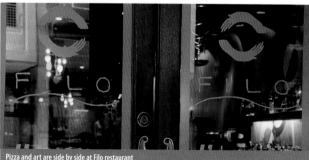
Pizza and art are side by side at Filo restaurant

business lunch spot – but the thinly sliced sashimi is divine.

🍴 **LE SUD** *French* $$$
☎ 4131-0130; Sofitel, Arroyo 841, Retiro; ⏱ 6:30-11am, 12:30-3pm, & 7:30pm-midnight; 🚍 93, 130, 152; ♿ Ⓥ
The award-winning chef at the Hotel Sofitel's buttoned-up French eatery, Thierry Pszonda, hails from Provence and his Mediterranean-influenced *plat du jour* is traditional enough to keep visiting Francophiles happy. Chandeliers and marble add a level of formality that's absent from the casual downtown brasseries.

🍴 **SIPAN** *Peruvian, Japanese* $$$
☎ 4315-0763; www.sipan.com.ar, in Spanish; Paraguay 624, Microcentro; ⏱ noon-4pm & 8pm-1am Mon-Sat; Ⓜ Line C San Martín
Japanese-Peruvian food is all the rage in Buenos Aires. Skip

the pretentious Palermo eateries peddling overpriced ceviche and taste-test the fresh, flavorful cuisine at Sipan. Tucked away in an unsuspecting shopping gallery, this low-lit pisco bar turns out imaginative seafood tapas, served heaping on ceramic spoons, and mouthwatering cocktails made with pisco the owners smuggled over from Peru.

🍸 **DRINK**

🍸 **CAFÉ RETIRO** *Cafe*
☎ 4516-0902; Estación Retiro (Retiro Station Lobby), Ramos Meija 1358, Retiro; ⏱ 6:30am-10pm; Ⓜ Line C Retiro; ♿ 🚻
Catching a train out of town? Allow an extra half-hour for coffee at this grand cafe in the main hall – the soaring ceilings, polished wood and bronze interior and bustling train station will make you feel like the star of a silent movie.

JORGE LUIS BORGES

Jorge Luis Borges (1899–1986) is Argentina's controversial literary hero. A linguist, poet and professor, Borges adored English literature – and though his countrymen chided him for being Anglocentric, he put his passion to practice and became a highly respected translator of Walt Whitman's poetry. Despite criticism from porteños and the cold shoulder from the Nobel Prize committee, Borges enjoyed popularity and acclaim abroad upon the publication of his short story collection *Labyrinths*, and literary scholars say that his handling of mythology and realism influenced many writers in Latin America, including Gabriel García Márquez. If you're near Plaza San Martín (p64), stroll past Maipú 994 and look up at the modest 6th-floor apartment where the literary legend lived and worked for a time.

Order a classic drink at the Marriott Plaza Bar

Y DADÁ *Bar, Restaurant*
☎ 4314-4787; San Martín 941, Retiro; ⊙ noon-2am Mon-Sat; Ⓜ Line C San Martín

The tiny bohemian Dadá, cluttered with wine bottles and with walls painted red, feels like an unassuming neighborhood bar in Paris. Get cozy with a varietal from a boutique bodega and order something savory off the bistro menu – the fresh guacamole and homemade potato chips are perfect for sharing – in this room full of easygoing waiters, intellectuals and groups of laughing friends.

Y MARRIOTT PLAZA BAR *Bar*
☎ 4318-3000; Basement, Marriott Plaza Hotel, Florida 1005, Retiro; ⊙ 11am-1am; Ⓜ Line C San Martín; ♿

Yeah, yeah – drinks at the Marriott doesn't sound like a winning cultural experience. But this palatial century-old hotel wasn't always part of the mainstream chain. Designed by Alfred Zucker, the man responsible for St Patrick's Cathedral in New York, it still boasts a genteel art-deco bar with cordial service and classic cocktails.

☆ PLAY

☆ ND/ATENEO *Concert Venue*
☎ 4328-2888; www.ndateneo.com.ar, in Spanish; Paraguay 918, Retiro; ⊙ box office noon-8pm Mon-Sat; 🚌 10, 21, 39, 102, 152; ♿

This gorgeous restored theater dates back to the 1930s. Best-known for hosting the Buenos Aires International Jazz Festival, the venue sees performances by tango legends and folk musicians on weekends. Get tickets from the box office or www.plateanet.com.

>SAN TELMO

Colorful San Telmo is a neighborhood in flux. Once an elegant colonial quarter of Spanish aristocrats, the barrio fell into near-ruin after the yellow fever epidemic of 1871 pushed the beau monde to higher ground and poor Italian immigrants turned the once-grand mansions into tenement housing. Porteños (BA locals) have long considered San Telmo – and its cobbled streets lined with dilapidated art-nouveau buildings, traditional *parrillas* (grill restaurants) and faded old cafes – to be run-down and dangerous. But thanks to sentimental locals and foreigners thrilled by the old-world atmosphere, money is pouring into the neighborhood. Even as sagging balconies are replaced, much of San Telmo's broken-down charm is alive and well in its crumbling facades and bohemian population. By day its narrow streets clamor with construction workers tripping across decaying sidewalks and tourists trolling the row of antique shops; at night, tango clubs fill with patrons and Plaza Dorrego throngs with a lighthearted crowd hanging around for cold *cerveza* (beer) and live music.

SAN TELMO

◉ SEE

El Zanjón de Granados ...1	C3
Museo Histórico	
Nacional 2	C5
Parque Lezama 3	C5
Plaza Dorrego 4	C4

◆ SHOP

Artesanos de Argentina ..5	C4
El Buen Orden 6	C3
Feria San Pedro Telmo ..(see 4)	
Ffiocca 7	B2
Gabriel del Campo	
Anticuario 8	C3
Gil Antigüedades 9	C4
HB Antiques 10	C4
La Cave de la Brigada ..11	B3
L'Ago 12	C3
L'Ago 13	C3
Materia Urbana 14	C3
Materia Urbana 15	C3

Mercado de San Telmo ..16	B3
Moebius 17	C5
Pablo Ramírez 18	B2
Puntos en el Espacio ...19	B3
Wussman 20	B2

🍴 EAT

Amici Miei 21	C4
Brasserie Petanque 22	C2
Café San Juan 23	B4
Comedor Nikkai 24	B3
El Desnivel 25	C3
Gran Parrilla del Plata .26	B3
La Brigada 27	B3
La Vieja Rotisería 28	C3
La Vinería de	
Gualterio Bolívar 29	B3
Manolo 30	B4
Origen 31	B4
Sagardi Euskal	
Taberna 32	C4
Taberna Baska 33	A3

🍸 DRINK

647 34	A3
Bar Británico 35	C5
Bar Plaza Dorrego ....(see 4)	
Bar Seddón 36	C3
Doppelgänger 37	B5
El Federal 38	B3
Gibraltar 39	B3
La Puerta Roja 40	B3
Pride Café 41	C3

★ PLAY

Bar Sur 42	C3
Centro Cultural	
Torquato Tasso 43	C5
Circo del Aire 44	B3
El Querandí 45	B2
El Viejo Almacén 46	C3
La Cumparsita 47	C3
La Trastienda 48	C2
Museum 49	B2

◉ SEE

◉ EL ZANJÓN DE GRANADOS

☎ 4361-3002; www.elzanjon.com.ar; Defensa 755, San Telmo; admission/tour $30, shorter tour on Sundays for $15; 🕙 11am-2pm Mon-Fri, 1-6pm Sun; 🚌 10, 20, 22, 29, 86; 🚻

Peek into the city's past at El Zanjón, an exquisitely restored urban villa and archeological site. Once the private residence of wealthy Spanish settlers, the abandoned mansion later became communal living space for immigrant families. In 1985, a local historian purchased the property and discovered a reservoir of antique treasures among the rubble in a series of underground tunnels. Today's tour guides lead visitors past the open-air water cistern and through the subterranean labyrinth, pointing out displays of French tiles, children's toys and other remnants of daily life in gentler times.

◉ MUSEO HISTÓRICO NACIONAL

☎ 4307-1182; cnr Defensa & Av Caseros, San Telmo; admission $4; 🕙 11am-5pm Tue-Fri, 3-6pm Sat & Sun, closed Jan; 🚌 29, 39, 53, 64

Housed in an old mansion on the edge of leafy Parque Lezama (right), this small museum offers an overview of Argentina's history. Displays of antique furniture, weaponry, clothing and artwork illustrate the nation's progress from the pre-Columbian era to independence.

◉ PARQUE LEZAMA

Defensa & Av Brasil, San Telmo; 🚌 10, 22, 29, 39; 🚻

Scruffy Parque Lezama was once thought to be the site of Buenos Aires' founding in 1536, but archeological teams recently refuted the hypothesis. Today's green park hosts old chess-playing gentlemen, bookworms toting *mate* (traditional Argentine tea) gourds and teenagers kissing on park benches. Don't miss the striking Iglesia Ortodoxa Rusa (Russian Orthodox Church) on the north side of the park.

FILETE PORTEÑO

It's said that while tango is an expression of sadness, *filete* — Buenos Aires' other folk art — is a celebration. Walk around San Telmo and you'll see the finely painted linework, curlicues and flowers of *filete*, a decorative painting style that emerged at the end of the 19th century as a form of distinguishing horse-drawn carts. The style moved to trucks and later to public buses, until the military government of 1976–83 outlawed *filete* on public transport. Today, several *fileteadores* (painters) sell works to tourists at craft markets. Also check out the new and beautiful *filete* buildings along Jean Jaurés, outside the Museo Casa Carlos Gardel (p108).

☉ PLAZA DORREGO
**Defensa & Humberto Primo, San Telmo;
🚍 10, 22, 29, 45, 86; ♿**
This vibrant colonial square, one of
the city's oldest, is a hub of activity.
Guitar-strumming artisans line
the plaza with displays of silver
jewelry and leather belts while
cafe-dwellers kick back at plastic
tables for conversation and tango
performances. Pull up a chair, order
a pitcher of sangria-like *clericot de
vino,* and ward off the parade of
magazine vendors with a polite but
firm '*no gracias*' (no, thank you).

SHOP

☐ ARTESANOS DE ARGENTINA
Souvenirs, Handicrafts
☎ 4300-5791; www.artesanosdesan
telmo.com.ar, in Spanish; Defensa 1281,
San Telmo; ⏱ 10am-7pm; 🚍 10, 22, 29
Support local artisans (and save a
few pesos) at this wonderful co-op
full of wooden dishes, hand-paint-
ed leather sandals, natural cigars,
dulce de leche liqueur and *mate*
gourds. The craftsmen are friendly
and eager to please at this large
store straddling Defensa.

☐ FERIA SAN PEDRO TELMO
Market
**Defensa, San Telmo; ⏱ 10am-6pm Sun;
🚍 10, 22, 29, 45, 86**
On Sundays, San Telmo's main
drag is closed to traffic and the
street is a sea of local families
and tourists browsing craft stalls,
waiting at vendor's carts for
freshly squeezed orange juice,
poking through the antique glass
ornaments on display on Plaza
Dorrego (left), and listening to
street performances by tango
orchestras.

☐ FFIOCCA *Women's Fashion*
☎ 4331-4585; www.ffiocca.com, in
Spanish; cnr Perú & Mexico, San Telmo;
⏱ 10:30am-7:30pm Mon-Fri, 10:30am-
3pm Sat; Ⓜ Line E Belgrano
High design meets ladylike
glamour at the boutique of
Florencia Fiocca, whose designs
have graced the dancers of Spain's
National Ballet (and Claire Danes
for an appearance in a Japanese
commercial). Her collection at this
airy corner shop features '40s-style
cocktail dresses, diaphanous summer sheaths and chic wool coats.

☐ GIL ANTIGÜEDADES
Antiques, Fashion
☎ 4361-5019; www.gilantiguedades
.com.ar; Humberto Primo 412, San
Telmo; ⏱ 11am-1pm & 3-7pm Tue-Sat,
11am-7pm Sun; 🚍 10, 22, 29, 45, 86
A window display of Great
Gatsby–style flapper dresses and
vintage nightgowns pulls passers-
by into San Telmo's finest antiques
emporium. Decorative objects
like china teapots and leather

hatboxes are overshadowed by the stunning array of silk slips and lacy Victorian gowns – John Galliano stopped by for inspiration on a recent visit to Buenos Aires.

🏠 LA CAVE DE LA BRIGADA
Wine

☎ 4362-2943; www.labrigada.com; Bolívar 1008, San Telmo; ❤ noon-4pm & 8pm-midnight; 🚌 10, 22, 24, 29, 45; ♿
This gem of a wine cellar stocks over 30,000 bottles. Do your future self a favor and pick up some Mora Negra de Finca las Moras 2003 – it'll be perfect to crack open when you're back home and staring, misty-eyed, at your vacation photos.

🏠 L'AGO *Home Decor, Souvenirs*
☎ 4362-3641; www.lagosantelmo.com; Defensa 919 & 970, San Telmo; ❤ 10am-8pm; 🚌 10, 22, 29, 45, 86
Kitschy-cool home decor, from fluorescent-hued *mate* sets to Frida Kahlo kitchen magnets, attracts hipsters and travelers to cute-as-a-button L'Ago. They have two stores located across the street from each other; don't miss buttery handmade soaps scented like chocolate, coffee and passion fruit.

🏠 MATERIA URBANA
Design, Home Decor

☎ 4361-5265; www.materiaurbana .com, in Spanish; Defensa 707, San Telmo; ❤ 10am-7pm Mon-Sat, 10am-8pm Sun; 🚌 10, 22, 29, 39, 86
This innovative design shop shows the work of over 100 local artists; one-of-a-kind finds include offbeat line drawings, abstract photography and jewelry made from silver, wood and coral. To accommodate the constant foot traffic, Materia Urbana recently expanded its store to include the corner space across the street on the Chile intersection.

A CABINET OF CURIOSITIES

San Telmo is famous for its myriad shops crammed with antiques, curios and collectibles. Poke around in these locales to find old-fashioned treasures from vintage suitcases to ivory busts and Bakelite bangles.

> **El Buen Orden** (☎ 15-5936-2820; Defensa 894; ❤ 11am-7pm) A charming little tangle of ladylike costume jewelry, antique ice skates and elbow-length opera gloves.
> **Gabriel del Campo Anticuario** (☎ 4361-2061; Defensa 990; ❤ 10am-7pm) Eclectic objects from antique tin toys to retro luggage.
> **HB Antiques** (☎ 4361-3325; www.hbantiques.com.ar; Defensa 1016; ❤ 10am-7pm Mon-Fri, 11am-5pm Sun) Classy art-deco antiques and paintings in a grand showroom.

Moebius boutique is waiting to dress you

MERCADO DE SAN TELMO
Market, Antiques

Defensa, Bolívar, Carlos Calvo & Estados Unidos block, San Telmo; ⏰ 10am-7pm; 🚌 10, 22, 29, 39, 86

Occupying an entire city block, this market was built in 1897 by Juan Antonio Buschiazzo, the same Italian-born Argentine architect who designed the Recoleta Cemetery (p93.) The wrought-iron interior and glass skylights make it one of BA's most atmospheric markets; it's also where locals shop for fresh produce, cheese and meat. Look for secondhand leather luggage, delicate wine decanters and Jackie O–style sunglasses at the peripheral antique stalls.

MOEBIUS *Women's Fashion*
☎ 4361-2893; **Defensa 1356, San Telmo;** ⏰ 3-8pm Wed-Sat, 11am-8:30pm Sun; 🚌 10, 22, 24, 29, 39

This funky little shop feels like the walk-in closet of the fashionable artist sister you never had: the racks are crowded with owner-designer Lilliana Zauberman's kaleidoscopic 1970s-style jersey dresses, whimsical ruffled bikinis, skirts printed with koi fish and frog patterns, cherry-red trench coats and handbags made from recycled materials.

PABLO RAMÍREZ *Fashion*
☎ 4342-7154; www.pabloramirez.com.ar; **Perú 586, San Telmo;** ⏰ 10:30am-7:30pm Mon-Fri, 10:30am-3pm Sat; Ⓜ Line E Belgrano

Stark black, crisp white and pared-down sophistication characterize the men's and women's collections by this venerated porteño (BA local) designer. A must-see for fashionistas who've strayed south from the Palermo boutique circuit.

PUNTOS EN EL ESPACIO
Fashion, Shoes

☎ 4307-1742; www.puntosenelespacio.com.ar; **Perú 979, San Telmo;** ⏰ 11am-8pm; 🚌 10, 22, 24, 29, 39

Racks of original edgy unisex collections by rising stars in the local fashion world line the walls of this concrete-floored space. Consider making a playful fashion statement with a pair of purple boots from the Hacer Pie line or a leather wallet lined with polka dot fabric. Also see the accessories-focused location on the corner of Defensa and Independencia.

🖪 WUSSMAN *Paper, Gifts*

☎ 4343-4707; Venezuela 570, San Telmo; 🕑 10:30am-8pm Mon-Fri; 10:30am-2pm Sat Ⓜ Line E Belgrano

Writers and artists delight in the gorgeous handmade paper at this chic art gallery and shop. Leather-bound journals, monogrammed stationery and oversized sketchbooks are made with recycled paper; the elegant restored house, now lined with brick and glass, also boasts an intriguing collection of rare books.

🍴 EAT

🍴 AMICI MIEI *Italian* $$$

☎ 4362-5562; www.amicimiei.com.ar, in Spanish; Defensa 1072, San Telmo; 🕑 11am-midnight Tue-Sun; 🚌 10, 22, 24, 29

There aren't many places in town where you can dine on gourmet black truffle carpaccio while an impeccably dressed tenor strides through the room crooning '*O Sole Mio*.' Try chef Sebastian Rivas Proia's exquisite tagliatelle with shrimp at a charming table for two overlooking Plaza Dorrego.

🍴 BRASSERIE PETANQUE

French $$

☎ 4342-7930; www.brasseriepetanque.com; cnr Defensa & Mexico, San Telmo; 🕑 noon-3:30pm Mon-Fri & Sun, 8:30pm-late Tue-Sat; 🚌 29, 93, 130, 152; 🚻 Ⓥ

This bright brasserie is a lively spot for Sunday brunch or a leisurely evening meal. Charismatic waiters pour complimentary aperitifs as you ponder steak tartare or roast chicken and peruse the short but wise list of wines by the glass. The *prix fixe* lunch menu is a steal.

🍴 CAFÉ SAN JUAN *Spanish* $$

☎ 4300-1112; Av San Juan 450, San Telmo; 🕑 noon-4pm & 8:30pm-midnight Tue-Sun; Ⓜ Line C San Juan; Ⓥ

Aside from the gleaming open kitchen, this petite restaurant isn't overly impressive to look at – the focus is firmly on the food at the family-run Café San Juan. A constantly changing chalkboard menu of tapas and main dishes is built around flavorful cheeses, seasonal vegetables like zucchini and eggplant and perfectly al dente pasta.

🍴 COMEDOR NIKKAI

Japanese $$

☎ 4300-5848; Av Independencia 732, San Telmo; 🕑 noon-3pm & 8-11pm Mon-Fri, 8pm-midnight Sat; Ⓜ Line C Independencia; Ⓥ

Forget sake cocktails and fashionable clientele – the calm, traditional

Comedor Nikkai, tucked away inside the Japanese Association's building, is worlds away from Palermo's stylish eateries. Join a low-key crowd here for steaming bowls of miso and fresh salmon rolls.

🍽 EL DESNIVEL *Parrilla* $

☎ 4300-9081; Defensa 855, San Telmo; 🕐 noon-4pm & 7:30pm-1am Tue-Sat, noon-1am Sun; 🚌 10, 22, 24, 29; ♿ 🍴

Eating at dirt-cheap Desnivel is a rite of passage. The convivial *parrilla* atmosphere is buoyed by deadpan waiters, a mix of hungry locals and eager tourists, the skill and speed of the overworked guys on the grill, and – of course – the affordable beef, sizzling *provoleta* (grilled provolone) and fried *empanadas*.

🍽 GRAN PARRILLA DEL PLATA *Parrilla* $$

☎ 4300-8858; cnr Chile & Perú, San Telmo; 🕐 noon-4pm & 8pm-late Mon-Sat, noon-late Sun; 🚌 10, 22, 24, 29; ♿ 🍴

Why forgo the appeal of a steakhouse just because you fancy a chunk of Brie in your salad and a 'real' wine glass? Fine cuts of meat and refined service make this corner *parrilla* a hit with the suits at lunchtime. When the weather's fine, grab a sidewalk table.

🍽 LA BRIGADA *Parrilla* $$$

☎ 4361-5557; www.labrigada.com; Estados Unidos 465, San Telmo; 🕐 noon-

3pm & 8pm-midnight Sun-Thu, 8pm-1am Fri & Sat; 🚌 10, 22, 24, 29; ♿

This classic San Telmo *parrilla* will almost certainly lose some of its neighborhood-style charm when it expands to include a much larger space next door. Still, the beef is brilliant – some dishes arrive so tender they're carved tableside with a spoon. Try the deep-fried vegetables and the deliciously antisocial *papas fritas provenzal* (garlic fries).

🍽 LA VIEJA ROTISERÍA *Parrilla* $

☎ 4362-5660; Defensa 963, San Telmo; 🕐 noon-4:30pm & 8pm-late; 🚌 10, 20, 22, 29; 🍴

Order the house wine served in a *pingüino* (penguin-shaped pitcher) and bump elbows with your fellow diners as you gobble steak and *chorizo* – it's all part of the experience at this no-frills *parrilla*. Thanks to bargain prices and a location near the entrance of the Mercado de San Telmo, the place often fills to capacity.

🍽 LA VINERÍA DE GUALTERIO BOLÍVAR *Modern Argentine, Spanish* $$$

☎ 4361-4709; www.lavineriadegual teriobolivar.com, in Spanish; Bolívar 865, San Telmo; 🕐 12:30-4pm & 9pm-midnight Tue-Sun; 🚌 10, 22, 24, 29; ♿ Ⓥ

Furnished in minimalist white and not much larger than a

studio apartment, La Vinería feels like a foodie's laboratory – fitting, considering the inventive molecular gastronomy that chef Alejandro Digilio concocts in the open kitchen. His cutting-edge eatery, which offers a nine-course tasting menu paired with several pours of high-end local wines, has attracted international attention since opening in 2007.

MANOLO Argentine $
☎ 4307-8743; www.restaurantmanolo .com.ar, in Spanish; cnr Cochabamba & Bolívar, San Telmo; ☷ noon-1am Tue-Sun; ☒ 10, 22, 24, 29; ♿ ♨
Honest local cuisine – steaks, salads and a huge menu of Spanish pastas and meat-and-potatoes platters – keep this friendly, family-run corner joint alive and kicking. The budget-friendly prices pull in neighborhood families and groups of hungry boys after *fútbol* practice.

ORIGEN Organic $
☎ 4362-7979; cnr Humberto Primo & Perú, San Telmo; ☷ noon-4pm Mon & Tue, noon-late Wed-Sun; ☒ 10, 20, 22, 29; ♿ Ⓥ ♨
Flying one of the only organic flags in this part of town, Origen is a bright, relaxed eatery with a short daily menu of fresh dishes like pumpkin ravioli and vegetable stir-fry with ginger. On a sunny day, you'll have to tussle with the locals for an outdoor table.

SAGARDI EUSKAL TABERNA Basque $$$
☎ 4361-2538; www.sagardi.com .ar; Humberto Primo 319, San Telmo; ☷ noon-4pm & 8pm-midnight; ☒ 10, 22, 24, 29; ♿ Ⓥ

Dine in style at Sagardi Euskal Taberna

This cavernous, striking new Basque eatery heralds San Telmo's gentrification. Swing by in the evening to pile your plate high with savory tapas and try the house *tempranillo* at the gorgeous, oversized communal wooden table in the front room.

🍴 TABERNA BASKA *Basque* $$
☎ 4334-0903; Chile 980; 🕐 noon-3:30pm & 8pm-late Tue-Sat, noon-3.30pm Sun; Ⓜ Line C Independencia
This long-standing, brightly lit Basque restaurant serves up down-home classics like *jamón iberico* and piping-hot paella to a crowd nostalgic for their Spanish mothers.

🍸 DRINK

🍸 647 *Bar, Restaurant*
☎ 4331-3026; www.club647.com; Tacuarí 647, San Telmo; 🕐 8pm-late Mon-Sat; Ⓜ Line C Independencia
This lavish Shanghai-style lounge boasts a talented barman and an experimental cocktail menu (try anything involving lychee fruit, but skip the margarita.) After-dinner drinks here are no bargain, especially by San Telmo standards, but shelling out the pesos is worth it for a chance to act posh in a plush, seductive space that feels like a designer opium den.

🍸 BAR BRITÁNICO *Cafe, Bar*
☎ 4361-2107; cnr Brasil & Defensa, San Telmo; 🕐 24hr; 🚌 10, 29, 39, 152; ♿

A classic corner cafe on the edge of Parque Lezama (p72), Bar Británico has an evocative old wooden interior and big glass windows that open to the street. Drop in for a *café cortado* (small espresso with milk) in the morning or a beer on a sunny afternoon.

🍸 BAR PLAZA DORREGO *Cafe, Bar*
☎ 4361-0141; cnr Defensa & Humberto Primo; 🕐 8am-3am; 🚌 24, 29, 130, 152; ♿
Despite the constant tourist presence, Bar Plaza Dorrego remains one of BA's most atmospheric watering holes. Take a load off to observe the tired but tuxedoed waiters making their rounds through an interior cluttered with antique bottles. Outdoors, back-packers knock back beer at rickety tables littered with peanut shells.

🍸 BAR SEDDÓN *Cafe, Bar*
☎ 4342-3700; cnr Chile & Defensa, San Telmo; 🕐 6pm-late Tue-Sun; 🚌 24, 29, 130, 152
This laid-back bar is outfitted with black-and-white tiles, rustic wood tables and the glow of hundreds of candles, and is housed in an old pharmacy. Drop in for an icy *chopp* (glass of draught beer) or for a late-night glass of red – you'll keep good company with a neighborhood crowd.

LEARNING LUNFARDO

Hearing some phrases on the street that your teacher never covered in Spanish 101? Forget looking them up in your pocket dictionary – you're hearing Lunfardo, a local dialect that developed in the early 20th century with influences ranging from jail slang and gaucho speak to the mishmash of languages spoken by French, Portuguese and Italian immigrants. The dialect was occasionally used in classic tango music, and today the language continues to thrive and grow – if you're listening for it, you'll hear *'Che, boludo'* (a casual form of address between friends, or alternatively, an insult) several times a day. Brush up on local lingo by mastering a few key words and phrases:

> *Pibe* – boy
> *Bondi* – bus
> *Re-copado* (adjective) and *una masa* (noun) – very cool
> *Que burra* – What a gorgeous woman
> *Ni en pedo* – I wouldn't do it even if I were drunk

� DOPPELGÄNGER
Bar, Restaurant
☎ 4300-0201; www.doppelganger.com
.ar; cnr Av Juan de Garay & Bolívar, San
Telmo; ☽ 7pm-1am Tue-Sat; Ⓜ Line C
San Juan; ♿

Forget Malbec and microbrews:
this new-on-the-scene speakeasy
celebrates the joy of a stiff martini.
An expert barman uses indigenous South American herbs to
spice up classic gin and vermouth
cocktails for the laid-back intellectual set. The cool 1930s decor
and huge black-and-white photographs pay homage to the barrio's
immigrant past.

☐br EL FEDERAL *Cafe, Bar*
☎ 4300-4313; cnr Perú & Carlos Calvo,
San Telmo; ☽ 8am-2am Mon-Thu, 8am-
4am Fri-Sun; 🚌 10, 20, 29, 86; ♿

El Federal's decorative wooden bar
and old-fashioned cash registers
are trappings of days gone by – the
well-loved corner joint has been
serving huge sandwiches and *cerveza artesanal* (hand-crafted beer)
under the glow of yellow lamplight
since 1864. Also check out the
newer La Poesía, El Federal's
literary-themed sister bar, on the
corner of Chile & Bolívar.

☐br GIBRALTAR *Bar, Restaurant*
☎ 4362-5310; Perú 895, San Telmo;
☽ 6pm-4am Mon-Fri, noon-4am Sat &
Sun; 🚌 10, 20, 29, 86

Porteños and expats hit this
English-style pub for icy pints,
pool tables, juicy burgers and
excellent ethnic dishes. Line up
at the bar to ask for a bowl of
Thai curry and a frosted glass of
whatever's on tap.

Monica Galan
Actress, Recipient of Silver Condor Award from Argentine Film Critics Association

Why do you love Buenos Aires? The people. When you need something, people help you. In European cities, the locals don't like tourists, but porteños are happy that you're here. **Favorite theater?** There are more theaters in Buenos Aires than in Paris. I like Teatro San Martín (p61). **Best classic Argentine film?** *Las Aguas Bajan Turbias* (River of Blood). It's about power and poverty. **Why live in San Telmo?** I love the variety of neighbors – artists, housewives, office workers. Nothing surprises us. I could leave the house with a melon on top of my head and no one would care. In Palermo, everyone's looking at the brand of your watch. **Favorite restaurant in the barrio?** Gran Parrilla del Plata (p77). **Where do you dance tango?** La Viruta (p125). **And watch tango?** La Cumparsita (p83). **Why is tango important?** It is the story, the heart, of Argentina. Tango music tells the truth.

NEIGHBORHOODS

SAN TELMO

▮ LA PUERTA ROJA Bar
☎ 4362-5649; Chacabuco 733, San Telmo; ◷ 6am-6am; Ⓜ Line C Independencia

A young crowd of pub crawlers and neighborhood kids climb the stairs to socialize and get sloshed at La Puerto Roja (the Red Door). This is a proper bar – no sweet cocktails or chalkboard wine list here – you'll be having a cold beer, vodka on the rocks or scotch, straight up.

▮ PRIDE CAFÉ Gay Cafe, Bar
☎ 4300-6435; Balcarce 869, San Telmo; ◷ 9am-9pm Mon-Fri, 11am-10pm Sat, 10am-8pm Sun; ▤ 10, 22, 29, 86; ♿

This cheerful, gay-friendly cafe serves up inexpensive breakfasts (think dulce de leche liqueur-smothered crepes and banana smoothies) to an eclectic crowd. Grab an Argentine fashion magazine and ask for the mouth-watering limonada con gengibre (lemonade with ginger).

★ PLAY

★ BAR SUR Tango
☎ 4362-6086; www.bar-sur.com.ar; cnr Estados Unidos & Balcarce, San Telmo; ◷ 8pm-late; ▤ 10, 22, 29, 86

Historic Bar Sur is one of the city's most celebrated, intimate (and expensive) tango show venues: you'll pay handsomely to sip champagne

THE FLYING TRAPEZE
A peek into the grand doorways and skinny alleys of San Telmo always yields a few surprises – a stray kitten sleeping in the sun, an old man painting at an easel, a flowering tree – but nothing will capture your attention like the trapeze artists and acrobats that practice in the neighborhood's cavernous studios. You can't help but stop and stare when you stumble upon a circus troupe setting up their tightrope inside a garage-like space that opens onto one of San Telmo's side streets. Keep your eye on Circo del Aire (☎ 4582-5309; Perú 856), a performance group that stages hipster circus shows on weekends and runs workshops teaching trapeze, acrobatics and 'aerial dance' to both adults and children.

at one of a dozen tables. Be prepared – the upscale dinner show is often participatory – so avoid it if you're not prepared to try a few tangled steps.

★ CENTRO CULTURAL TORQUATO TASSO
Tango, Live Music
☎ 4307-6506; www.torquatotasso.com.ar, in Spanish; Defensa 1575, San Telmo; ◷ shows 10pm Tue-Sat; ▤ 10, 22, 93, 130

Serious tango musicians, both established and up-and-coming, perform at this well-respected venue just off Parque Lezama.

⭐ EL QUERANDÍ *Tango*

☎ 4345-1770; www.querandi.com.ar;
Perú 302, Montserrat; 🕓 dinner 8pm,
show 10pm; Ⓜ Line E Bolívar; ♿

By day, El Querandí is an upscale
restaurant serving salmon to
businessmen – by night, the space
is completely blackened for its
famous tango dinner shows. These
are stylish, slick, sexy and professional. And very popular –
bookings essential.

⭐ EL VIEJO ALMACÉN
Tango

☎ 4307-7388; www.viejoalmacen.com,
in Spanish; cnr Balcarce & Av Independencia, San Telmo; 🕓 dinner from 8pm,
show 10pm; 🚌 10, 29, 93 130, 152; ♿

This polished tango show, put
on nightly in one of San Telmo's
old colonial homes, incorporates
indigenous music and dance
to the usual routine. It's widely
considered one of the best shows
in the city – but avoid dining at
the generic restaurant of the same
name, located just across the
street.

⭐ LA CUMPARSITA
Tango, Live Music

☎ 4361-6880; www.lacumparsitatango
.com.ar; Chile 302, San Telmo; 🕓 8pm-
late; 🚌 10, 22, 29, 86, 126

This low-key tango bar hosts a
legion of excellent musicians and
vocalists, dancing duos, and an
appealing mix of locals and
tourists coming in from the street
to drink wine in the intimate
wood-paneled space.

⭐ LA TRASTIENDA *Live Music*

☎ 4342-7650; www.latrastienda.com,
in Spanish; Balcarce 460, San Telmo;
admission prices vary; 🕓 from 6pm
Mon-Sun; 🚌 24, 29, 86, 130;

This happening live-music venue
hosts acts from Latin America and
beyond – highly anticipated gigs
have included Damien Rice, Kevin
Johansen and the Nada, Bright
Eyes and Argentine-born indie
darling José Gonzalez. The theater
has standing room for up to 1000
downstairs and another 350 seats
on the upper level.

⭐ MUSEUM *Dance Club*

☎ 4771-9628; www.museumclub.com
.ar, in Spanish; Perú 535, San Telmo;
🕓 8pm-2am Wed, 10pm-late Fri-Sun;
Ⓜ Line E Belgrano; ♿

The striking steel building that
houses Museum was designed
by Gustave Eiffel (yes, the same
French architect who made an
indelible mark on the Parisian
skyline), though what transpires
inside isn't quite as romantic – on
Wednesday nights, the dark, lofty
interior is a full-blown meat market
as the macho 'after office' crowds
loosen their ties and get rowdy
over strong cocktails.

>LA BOCA

Any student of the Spanish language can translate the name of this rough-and-tumble southern neighborhood: La Boca means 'the mouth,' a reference to the barrio's location at the mouth of the Riachuelo. The working-class Italian immigrants who settled around the port during the mid-19th century left a powerful legacy – they 'borrowed' ship paint to decorate their ramshackle houses, creating the vibrantly hued stretch now known as Caminito, and, along with their neighboring Spaniards, Africans and gauchos, they invented tango. Today, many porteños (BA locals) avoid La Boca, criticizing its dirty river, dangerous side streets and the violent *futból* fans who frequent La Bombonera stadium. But La Boca is on the upswing – the cutting-edge Proa art gallery has undergone a major renovation, and foreigners still flock here to see the colorful houses and campy tango performers. The tourist spectacle can be cheesy, and the neighborhood surrounding Caminito isn't safe to wander around, especially at night. But the old port and the city's south hold a certain romance that didn't escape tango composers like Fernando Solanas, who wrote 'I carry the South like a destiny of my heart/I am from the South like the melodies of the *bandoneón*.'

LA BOCA

◎ SEE
Caminito 1 B5
Fundación Proa 2 B5
Museo de Bellas Artes de La
   Boca Benito
   Quinquela Martín 3 C5
Museo de la Pasión
   Boquense 4 B4

⌂ SHOP
Centro Cultural de los
   Artistas 5 B5

ⓘ EAT
El Obrero 6 C3
Il Matterello 7 B4

★ PLAY
Estadio Alberto J Armando
   (La Bombonera) 8 B4

SEE

CAMINITO

🚌 29, 64; ♿

La Boca's most famous street is a tangle of brightly painted houses, local artists selling splashy paintings of BA's tourist sites, and flashy tango dancers twirling for a camera-snapping audience. The surrounding stalls offer generally high-quality crafts (with prices to match). Also see p18.

FUNDACIÓN PROA

☎ 4104-1000; www.proa.org; Av Don Pedro de Mendoza 1929, La Boca; admission $10; 🕐 11am-8pm Tue-Sun; 🚌 29, 53, 64, 152; ♿

After a well-executed renovation, this contemporary art gallery and foundation is almost too cool for La Boca. Each year, Proa hosts six temporary shows from Argentina and abroad, as well as workshops, courses, conferences and concerts. The sophisticated cafe on the top level stands in high contrast to the surrounding barrio. See also p18.

MUSEO DE BELLAS ARTES DE LA BOCA BENITO QUINQUELA MARTÍN

☎ 4301-1080; Av Don Pedro de Mendoza 1835, La Boca; admission $1; 🕐 10am-5pm Tue-Fri, 11am-5:30pm Sat & Sun, closed Jan; 🚌 29, 64, 152; ♿

Argentine painter Benito Quinquela Martín (1890–1977) lived and

MAGIC BUS

So you want to go on an authentic city bus tour (the kind that's free of air conditioning and camera-wielding tourists?) Depart from La Boca on public bus 29 – the main stop is at the bottom of El Caminito – for an unforgettable ride through the city with a colorful cast of local characters and a moody bus driver at the helm. The rusty *colectivo* (bus) leaves La Boca and barrels through San Telmo (p70), around the Casa Rosada (p38), along Av de Mayo to Av 9 de Julio and right by the Obelisco (p40), then past the imposing Palacio de las Aguas Corrientes (p54). After the bumpy ride, you'll want to get off at Plaza Italia in Palermo and head to a park for some peace and quiet or to one of Palermo Viejo's cool eateries for drinks and dinner.

worked in this huge, boxy waterfront building before donating it to the government in 1936; these days, the structure houses a museum showing the work of national artists like Berni and Soldi, and, more significantly, an outstanding collection of Martín's own colorfully painted depictions of La Boca.

MUSEO DE LA PASIÓN BOQUENSE

☎ 4362-1100; www.museoboquense .com, in Spanish; Brandsen 805, La Boca; admission $12; 🕐 10am-7pm, closed on game days; 🚌 10, 29, 64; ♿

No visit to La Boca is complete without visiting this slick museum

Don't miss the colorful world of the Caminito

and shrine to the Boca Juniors football club. Petrified of braving the volatile stadium crowds? Step inside a giant soccer ball, where a 360-degree movie screen transports you into a crowd-filled stadium – not as exciting as the real thing, but close.

SHOP

CENTRO CULTURAL DE LOS ARTISTAS *Art, Handicrafts*
☎ 4301-1080; Magallanes 861, La Boca; ⏱ 10am-6pm; 🚌 29, 64

While the area around El Caminito is jammed with dozens of markets and shops hawking crafts and souvenirs, this complex was the first and remains the best. Not only does it give you an opportunity to peek inside one of the former tenements, but it also has a small art gallery where you can buy local paintings.

EAT

EL OBRERO *Parrilla $*
☎ 4362-9912; Agustín Caffarena 64, La Boca; ⏱ noon-4pm & 8pm-midnight Mon-Sat; 🚌 29, 64, 86, 130; 👶

Ironically, the exterior of BA's most famous *bodegón* (workers' cafe; *obrero* translates as workers or working-class) is often illuminated by the flash of paparazzi bulbs as local celebrities pull up for high-profile dinners of roasted

ribs and *milanesa* (fried steak). If your limo doesn't arrive after dinner, don't be tempted to walk – take a taxi, La Boca's a tough 'hood.

IL MATTERELLO *Italian $$*
☎ 4307-0529; Martín Rodríguez 517, La Boca; ⏱ 12:30-3pm & 8:30pm-midnight Tue-Sat, 12:30-3pm Sun, closed Jan; 🚌 29, 64, 86, 152; 👶

This simple, attractively furnished La Boca eatery specializes in homemade pastas tossed with classic Italian sauces like *carbonara* and *puttanesca*. The service is spotty, but the tiramisú is delicious.

THE EMPANADA TRAIL

First prize for fantastic and fuss-free finger food goes to Argentina. *Empanadas*, baked (or sometimes fried) pastries stuffed with meat or cheese, are the go-to snack for porteños – when they're having a few friends over for drinks, they'll order a box from the local *empanaderia*. The shape of each pastry is cleverly chosen to indicate the filling inside; the most popular pockets are *carne* (minced meat), *carne picante* (spicy minced meat), *cebolla y queso* (onion and cheese), *jamón y queso* (ham and cheese), *humita* (creamed corn) and *caprese* (tomato, basil, and mozzarella.) Packing a picnic? Just look for an *empanaderia* that's busy with locals – porteños are fanatical about where they buy these savory specialties.

DIEGO ARMANDO MARADONA

In recent years, he's made the headlines for drug addiction and heart attacks, but back in his glory days, Diego Armando Maradona was the populist hero of Argentina. Along with Brazilian Pelé, Maradona's considered the greatest *fútbol* (soccer) player ever to grace the turf. Born in 1960 in a Buenos Aires shantytown, Diego made his professional debut for Argentinos Juniors in 1976 at the age of 15. He transferred to his favorite club, Boca Juniors, in 1981, finally ending up with SSC Napoli (and making a record salary) in 1984. But it was playing for Argentina that made Maradona a superstar. His two goals in the World Cup quarter-final against England in 1986 are legendary football moments. With the first, he surreptitiously punched the ball into goal, later claiming it was 'La Mano de Dios' ('The Hand of God') that helped him. With the second goal, Diego bamboozled the entire English defense in what was later named the 'Goal of the Century.' Maradona left Napoli in 1992, after a 15-month ban for failing a drug test for cocaine, and was sent home from the 1994 World Cup for testing positive to ephedrine. It has been widely reported that his health remains fragile. News of the soccer star makes almost as many headlines today as his brilliant but beleaguered football career once did.

 PLAY

⭐ **LA BOMBONERA** Sport

☎ 4362-2260; www.bocajuniors.com
.ar, in Spanish; Estadio Alberto J Armando
(La Bombonera), Brandsen 805, La Boca;
admission free on non-game days;
🕙 varies, check website for details;
🚌 29, 64, 86, 152

Watching a football game at this La Boca stadium is an experience. The stands are so rickety that the whole thing rocks when fans jump up and down, singing songs of abuse to the other side. Consider venturing toward the Boca Juniors' home turf through a tour operator like Tangol (www.tangol .com) – matches can be more than a little unruly. See also p12.

>RECOLETA & BARRIO NORTE

Old money abounds in Recoleta. The city's wealthiest citizens relocated here as the yellow fever epidemic ravaged San Telmo in 1871, and this north-of-center area developed to suit the refined tastes of the Spanish elite. Many members of the original high society never left the neighborhood – they're buried in grand fashion in the magnificent Cementerio de la Recoleta, and their aesthetic contributions live on. This is the city's most Parisian quarter, featuring wide avenues, belle-epoque apartment buildings and beautifully landscaped parks. Swanky Av Alvear is dripping with diamonds – opulent hotels like the Alvear Place roll out the red carpet for distinguished guests while exclusive boutiques sell sapphires to rich porteñas (BA locals) toting tiny dogs. While Recoleta's natives are a conservative set, a more diverse population streams out of bookstores and ice-cream shops on Av Santa Fe in nearby Barrio Norte, where dozens of old mansions have been converted into restaurants and bars.

RECOLETA & BARRIO NORTE

⊙ SEE
Basílica de Nuestra
  Señora del Pilar 1 D2
Biblioteca Nacional 2 C1
Cementerio de la
  Recoleta 3 D2
Centro Cultural
  Recoleta 4 D2
Daniel Abate 5 B2
Floralis Genérica 6 D1
Isabel Anchorena 7 F3
Museo Nacional de
  Bellas Artes 8 D1
Museo Xul Solar 9 B3
Palais de Glace 10 E1
Praxis 11 E3

🏠 SHOP
Airedelsur 12 E2
A.Y. Not Dead 13 F3

Buenos Aires Design 14 D2
El Ateneo Grand
  Splendid 15 D4
El Fenix 16 F4
Etiqueta Negra 17 F2
Feria de Artesanos
  de Plaza Francia 18 D1
Josefina Ferroni 19 F3
Patio Bullrich 20 F2
Rossi & Caruso 21 E4
Tealosophy 22 E2
Tramando 23 E2

🍴 EAT
788 Food Bar 24 D3
Cumaná 25 D4
Gran Bar Danzon 26 F3
La Bourgogne 27 E2
L'Orangerie .... (see 27)
Oviedo 28 B3

🍸 DRINK
Buller Pub & Brewery ..29 D2
Clásica y Moderna 30 D4
La Biela 31 E2
Milión 32 E4

⭐ PLAY
Basement Club 33 D3
Glam 34 A4
Notorious 35 D4

◑ SEE

◉ BASÍLICA DE NUESTRA SEÑORA DEL PILAR

☎ 4803-6793; www.basilicadelpilar .org.ar, in Spanish; Junín 1904, Recoleta; admission free; ☾ 8am-9pm; 🚌 10, 17, 60, 92, 110; ♿

Yes, that's a pair of skulls on your right as you enter the basilica. But the centerpiece of this gleaming white colonial church, built by Jesuits in 1716, is a Peruvian altar adorned with silver from Argentina's northwest. The crypt leads into underground tunnels that once connected the basilica to other sections of the city. Free tours in English and Spanish start at 10:30am and 6:15pm Monday to Saturday.

◉ BIBLIOTECA NACIONAL

☎ 4808-6000; www.bibnal.edu.ar, in Spanish; Agüero 2502, Recoleta; admission free; ☾ 9am-8pm Mon-Fri, noon-7pm Sat & Sun; 🚌 10, 21, 37, 38, 41, 59, 60, 93, 110; ♿

Sixties-style concrete meets futuristic design at the imposing National Library, conceived by famed architect Clorinda Testa and standing on the site where Eva and Juan Perón once lived. Evita died here in 1952, and the home was later razed by the post-

Check out the street art at Centro Cultural Recoleta

LITTLE EVA

The short life of the iconic Eva María Duarte de Perón was like a Cinderella story with a dark twist of an ending. The small-town girl left home at the tender age of 15 and moved to the big city, where she worked, and often struggled to make ends meet, as a radio actress. At 24, she met Juan Perón, a politician twice her age, at a fundraiser. Their fast and furious courtship culminated with Perón's election to the Argentine presidency in 1946. As the nation's charismatic first lady, Evita (little Eva) was a feminist and philanthropist who campaigned tirelessly for the city's poor. The porteño working class adored her, though her critics often point to the sharp contrast between her political platform and her glamorous, European-designer-label-wearing image. Eva had bigger problems to contend with, however, as the public denounced the president's dictatorial style, the military staged a coup against her husband, and, to top it off, she was diagnosed with cancer. Evita died at age 33, and while she remains a tragic character in foreigners' imaginations, the local perception of the Perón legacy is darker and more complex, wrapped up in the memory of the bloody political and social events that followed Eva's premature death.

Perón government, but a stylized statue at the foot of the hill pays tribute to the former first lady.

CEMENTERIO DE LA RECOLETA

☎ 4803-1594; www.cementeriorecoleta .com.ar; Junín 1790, Recoleta; admission free; ⏱ 7am-6pm, check blackboard for free English tour times; 🚌 10, 17, 60, 92, 110; ♿

Visitors come to this famous cemetery to make the pilgrimage to Evita's tomb, but the labyrinthine necropolis is a destination in itself. Explore the final resting place of some of the country's most influential figures – politicians, educators, artists – with a tour guide, or just get lost among the stray cats and cobwebs of the cemetery's shadowy passageways. See also p11.

CENTRO CULTURAL RECOLETA

☎ 4803-1040; www.centrocultural recoleta.org, in Spanish; Junín 1930, Recoleta; admission by donation; ⏱ 2-9pm Mon-Fri, 10am-9pm Sat & Sun; 🚌 10, 17, 60, 92, 110; ♿

Sandwiched between Buenos Aires Design (p95) and the Basílica de Nuestra Señora del Pilar (opposite), this one-time Franciscan convent is now one of the city's most dynamic cultural centers. The spacious rooms and old-fashioned archways make a picturesque setting for excellent sculpture, photography and video exhibits, while the sweeping terrace hosts live jazz performances.

GALLERY WALK

Upscale Recoleta is the epicenter of the city's art scene. If you fancy a little hobnobbing with porteño painters and the rich patrons who support them – while sipping free champagne, of course – keep your eye out for events and openings at these galleries.

> **Daniel Abate** (☎ 4804-8247; www.danielabategaleria.com.ar; Pasaje Bollini 2170; ⏱ noon-7pm Tue-Sat) Edgy, youthful visual arts exhibits in an unpretentious setting.
> **Isabel Anchorena** (☎ 4811-5335; www.galeriaisabelanchorena.sion.com; Arenales 1239; ⏱ 11am-8pm Mon-Fri & 11am-1pm Sat) This old-school gallery represents dozens of talents in the realm of sculpture, photography and painting.
> **Praxis** (☎ 4813-8639; www.praxis-art.com; Arenales 1311; ⏱ 10:30am-8pm Mon-Fri & 10:30am-2pm Sat) Contemporary Latin American art with an international reach – Praxis also has spaces in Miami and New York.

◎ FLORALIS GENÉRICA
Plaza Naciones Unidas, Recoleta; 🚌 **12, 124, 130;** ♿
This gargantuan solar-powered flower sculpture is the inspired creation of architect Eduardo Cata-lano, who designed and funded the project in 2002. Check out the stunning Floralis Genérica at dawn, when its enormous metallic petals open to the sun, or at dusk, when the flower delicately closes for the night.

◎ MUSEO NACIONAL DE BELLAS ARTES
☎ **4803-8814; www.aamnba.com.ar; Av del Libertador 1473, Recoleta; admission free;** ⏱ **12:30-7:30pm Tue-Fri, 9:30am-7:30pm Sat & Sun;** 🚌 **17, 67, 92, 93, 130;** ♿
The country's most important fine-arts museum boasts an extensive collection of 19th- and 20th-century Argentine and indigenous art, as well as works by European masters such as Renoir, Rodin, Monet, Toulouse-Lautrec, Gauguin, Rembrandt and Van Gogh.

◎ MUSEO XUL SOLAR
☎ **4824-3302; www.xulsolar.org.ar; Laprida 1212, Recoleta; admission $3;** ⏱ **noon-7:30pm Tue-Fri, noon-7pm Sat** Ⓜ **Line D Agüero**
How could you *not* be curious about a man who created his own language and claimed to live in his own private time zone? This museum exhibits the unusual artwork and inventions of the avant-garde painter, musician, writer and mathematician Ale-jandro Xul Solar (1887–1963). A friend of Borges, he dabbled in fields as diverse as astrology and philosophy.

⊙ PALAIS DE GLACE

www.palaisdeglace.org, in Spanish;
Posadas 1725, Recoleta; admission free,
tours & exhibits $10; ☺ noon-8pm Tue-
Fri, 10am-8pm Sat & Sun ☒ 17, 61, 92,
93, 130; ♿

The name (and circular shape) give
it away – the Palais de Glace was
once the ice-skating rink of BA's
high society. The glamorous belle-
epoque structure, built in 1910,
also served as a tango ballroom
before being declared a National
Monument in 2004. Now the landmark building exhibits visual arts;
on weekend afternoons, guided
tours of the building (in English)
start at 5pm (bookings required).

🛍 SHOP

🏠 AIREDELSUR
Home Decor, Handicrafts

☎ 4803-6100; www.airedelsur.com; Av
Alvear 1833 #1129, Recoleta; ☺ 10am-
8pm Mon-Fri, 10am-2pm Sat; ☒ 17, 59,
67, 75, 102

The rustic chic airedelsur label
was beloved by porteños long
before it was featured in *Vogue*.
Designer Marcelo Lucini collabo-
rates with Argentine craftsmen to
create stunningly original home
decor made with alpaca silver,
wood, onyx and other all-natural
materials. Queen Rania of Jordan
reportedly picked up more than
200 pieces for her palaces.

🏠 A.Y. NOT DEAD *Fashion*

☎ 4815-7954; www.aynotdead.com
.ar; Parera 175, Recoleta; ☺ 11am-7pm
Mon-Sat; ☒ 17, 59, 67, 75, 102

Half street, half punk, A.Y. Not
Dead always makes a splash at
BA's biannual Fashion Week (p25).
Peruse the edgy collection of
weathered denim skinny jeans,
graphic jersey tanks and rain-
bow-hued vinyl miniskirts at the
Recoleta branch of this youthful
fashion house.

🏠 BUENOS AIRES DESIGN
Home Decor, Design

☎ 5777-6000; www.designrecoleta
.com.ar; Av Pueyrredón 2501, Recoleta;
☺ 10am-9pm; ☒ 10, 17, 60, 92, 110

This chic contemporary design
center bustles with dozens of
stores specializing in minimalist
furniture, high-tech lighting and
sophisticated home decor. Pop
into the airy Morph boutique for
snazzy wine decanters and leather
breakfast trays.

🏠 EL ATENEO GRAND SPLENDID
Books, Music

☎ 4813-6052; Av Santa Fe 1860,
Recoleta; ☺ 9am-10pm Mon-Sat, noon-
10pm Sun; Ⓜ Line D Callao

Though part of the El Ateneo
chain, this is no ordinary bookstore – the Grand Splendid oc-
cupies a fabulous antique cinema

El Ateneo Grand Splendid (p95), possibly the most spectacular bookshop in the world

and theater where Carlos Gardel, Argentina's iconic tango legend, crooned on stage to an adoring crowd. Today, bookshelves crowd the mezzanine. Relive the theatrical magic with coffee on the 1920s-style stage.

🏠 EL FENIX Wine, Deli
☎ 4811-0363; Av Santa Fe 1199, Retiro;
🕐 8am-8pm Mon-Fri, 8am-2pm Sat;
🚌 10, 21, 39, 67, 152
An excellent city wine shop. Name your preferences and price range, then put the knowledgeable staff to the test.

🏠 ETIQUETA NEGRA
Men's Fashion
☎ 5777-6769; Posadas 1229, Recoleta;
🕐 10am-9pm; 🚌 17, 59, 67, 75, 102

This stylish menswear label specializes in dapper Italian wool suits, cool leather jackets and slim-cut wool sweaters in dark shades of charcoal and black. The look mixes a contemporary sensibility with classic tailoring.

🏠 FERIA DE ARTESANOS DE PLAZA FRANCIA Market
www.feriaplazafrancia.com; Plaza Francia, Recoleta; 🕐 11am-8pm Sat & Sun; 🚌 10, 17, 60, 92, 110
On sunny weekend afternoons, this upscale craft market teems with artisans selling exquisite bronze jewelry, brightly colored cotton sundresses and hand-woven clutch purses. The sprawling display enlivens the green slope of Plaza Francia.

JOSEFINA FERRONI
Shoes

☎ 5811-1951; www.josefinaferroni
.com.ar; Arenales 1278, Recoleta; ⏱ 2-
8pm Mon, 11am-8pm Tue-Sat; 🚌 10, 21,
39, 67, 152

Argentina's answer to Jimmy
Choo. The old-school glamour and
coquettish colors of these gor-
geously crafted boots, platform
heels and open-toed flats have
earned Josefina Ferroni countless
porteña fans and growing international exposure.

PATIO BULLRICH
Shopping Mall

☎ 4814-7400/7500; www.shopping
bullrich.com.ar; Av del Libertador 750,
Recoleta; ⏱ 10am-9pm; 🚌 17, 61, 62,
92, 124, 130

Patio Bullrich is the place where
posh porteños part with their
pesos; expect international luxury

brands like Salvatore Ferragamo
alongside exclusive local design
shops and upscale cafes.

ROSSI & CARUSO *Leather*

☎ 4811-1538; www.rossicaruso.com; Av
Santa Fe 1601, Recoleta; ⏱ 9:30am-8pm
Mon-Fri, 10am-7pm Sat; 🚌 17, 59, 67,
75, 102

Should you be in the market for
a fine leather saddle or a serious
gaucho knife, you've come to the
right place. The leather goods
here, from knee-high riding boots
to belts and bags, are beautifully
made.

TRAMANDO
Fashion, Home Decor

☎ 4811-0465; www.tramando
.com; Rodríguez Peña 1973, Recoleta;
⏱ 10:30am-8:30pm Mon-Fri, 11am-7pm
Sat; 🚌 17, 59, 67, 92

Designer Martín Churba is a highly
respected name on the local and

TEA FOR TWO

Following in the grand tradition of Londoners and society ladies, porteñas have taken
to the ritual of afternoon tea. Which isn't to say that *mate* is on its way out, mind you –
taking a break for chamomile and crumpets is just another excuse for these highly social
souls to get together and discuss whether or not the president has had plastic surgery. If
you're short on time, pick up the trendiest tea leaves in town at the charming **Tealosophy**
(☎ 4804-7020; www.tealosophy.com; Av Alvear 1883 #37; ⏱ 10:30am-8pm Mon-Sat).
Have an hour or two to spare? Take your tea in style at the lavish **L'Orangerie** (☎ 4808-
2949; www.alvearpalace.com; Alvear Palace Hotel, Av Alvear 1891; ⏱ 4:30pm Mon-Sat
& 5pm Sun), where white-gloved service and impossibly elegant little cakes await guests
fond of old-fashioned pleasantries.

...hion circuit. His ...o-friendly collec-...pattern, texture, ...led fabrics and the occasional indigenous textile.

EAT

788 FOOD BAR
Modern Argentine $$

☎ 4814-4788; www.788food-bar.com .ar, in Spanish; Arenales 1877, Barrio Norte; ⏱ 10am-2am Mon-Sat; Ⓜ Line D Callao; 🚌 10, 39, 60; Ⓥ ♿

Foodies and cocktail connoisseurs alike rave about 788 Food Bar: an insulated bread box is delivered to your table on arrival, the fusion cuisine is simple and gourmet and the mixed drinks served in the up-stairs lounge are superb. Best of all is the (reverse) sticker shock: the set lunch menu hardly costs more than a taxi ride across town.

CUMANÁ
Northern Argentine $

☎ 4813-9207; Rodriguez Peña 1149, Recoleta; ⏱ noon-1am; 🚌 10, 39, 152; ♿ Ⓥ ♿

This bright, upbeat eatery is one of the only places in town serving traditional dishes from far-flung provinces of Argentina. The hearty *criollo* (Spanish/Indian) cuisine baking in the adobe oven includes *locro,* a thick corn-based stew made with meat and vegetables. Don't miss the *humita,* a creamy cheese and corn mixture wrapped up in corncob leaves.

GRAN BAR DANZON
International $$

☎ 4811-1108; www.granbardanzon .com.ar; Libertad 1161, Retiro; ⏱ 7pm-late, from 8pm Sat & Sun; 🚌 10, 39, 67, 102, 152; Ⓥ

Gran Bar Danzon is the kind of place you drop by with the intention of trying a glass of wine or two with friends – but thanks to the cool urban atmosphere, you're still there four hours later, sampling sushi and confit of duck and pretending not to stare at the parade of pretty people squeezing past your table.

LA BOURGOGNE
French $$$

☎ 4808-2100; www.alvearpalace.com; Alvear Palace Hotel, Av Alvear 1891, Recoleta; ⏱ noon-3:30pm & 7:30pm-midnight Mon-Sat; 🚌 67, 93, 130; ♿

This cultivated, classy French res-taurant at the Alvear Palace Hotel sees sommeliers gliding through hushed rooms as chef Jean Paul Bondoux creates courses and set menus centered on caviar, fish and rabbit. The adjacent Taste Vins cel-lar also hosts wine tastings (p16).

OVIEDO *Spanish* $$$

☎ 4822-5415; www.oviedoresto.com .ar, in Spanish; Beruti 2602, Barrio Norte;

☾ noon-3:30pm, 8pm-1am; Ⓜ Line D Pueyrredón; Ⓥ

The sole and sea bass at Oviedo are so fresh they're practically still flopping around. Prepared with contemporary Spanish flair and paired with cold white wine, fish takes center stage at this fine dining institution –although melt-in-your-mouth pork dishes are also worth writing home about.

DRINK

Ⓨ BULLER PUB & BREWERY
Bar

☎ 4808-9061; www.bullerpub .com; Roberto M Ortiz 1827, Recoleta; ☾ noon-late; 🚌 17, 61, 62, 93, 110; ♿

Beer connoisseurs will welcome the sight of the stainless-steel tanks above the bar. Be merry with tasty microbrews like the delicious Honey Beer or the refreshing India Pale Ale.

Ⓨ CLÁSICA Y MODERNA
Cafe, Bar

☎ 4812-8707; www.clasicaymoderna .com, in Spanish; Av Callao 892, Recoleta; ☾ 8am-1am Mon-Wed, 8am-3am Fri & Sat; Ⓜ Line D Callao; ♿

Mingle with an arty, intellectual crowd at this good-looking 'multi-espacio' (it's a cafe, bar, restaurant, art space, bookstore and music venue all rolled into one).

Both classic and modern – hence the name – it fills to capacity for jazz performances and poetry readings.

Ⓨ LA BIELA *Cafe*

☎ 4804-0449; www.labiela.com; Av Quintana 600, Recoleta; ☾ 7am-late; 🚌 10, 17, 60, 92, 110; ♿ ♨

There's no need to squabble over a few outdoor tables: La Biela's huge patio, shaded by the leafy branches of a formidable *gomero* (rubber) tree, has enough sidewalk seating for the entire national *fútbol* team (and their dear mothers, too). Take a break from sightseeing with coffee at this refined corner institution just off Plaza Francia.

Ⓨ MILIÓN *Bar*

☎ 4815-9925; www.milion.com.ar; Paraná 1048, Barrio Norte; ☾ noon-2am Mon-Wed, noon-3am Thu, noon-4am Fri, 8pm-late Sat & Sun; 🚌 10, 29, 39, 102, 152

True to its name, Milión looks like a million dollars – the restored mansion comprises a gorgeous open-air courtyard brightened by twinkle lights and a grand outdoor staircase that leads to the upper-level bar. Pretty young things sprawling on the moonlit steps, sipping frozen mojitos and basil daiquiris, complete the picture.

Ricardo Arenaza
Sommelier

What's so great about Argentine wine? We're part of the 'new world' of wine. The 'old world' – France, Italy – is limited by rules, but we, like Chileans and Australians, are free to design different styles of wine. Of course we also have vineyards at high altitude, pure mountain water, a dry climate and plenty of sunshine. **Why has the quality of national wine improved so much in recent years?** Foreign investors and wine experts brought their ideas and impressions to Argentina. Now Malbec is a phenomenon, like the internet, a new language that everyone wants to speak. **City's best wine shop?** Lo de Joaquin Alberdi (p117.) **Best bottle under $30?** Norton D.O.C., a Malbec from Luján de Cuyo. **Which restaurant has the best wine selection?** Oviedo (p98) has a great cellar. I like Gran Bar Danzon (p98) too.

⭐ PLAY

⭐ BASEMENT CLUB
Dance Club

☎ 4812-3584; www.theshamrockbar
.com; Rodríguez Peña 1220, Recoleta;
🕒 midnight-late, depending on event;
Ⓜ Line D Callao; 🚌 10, 21, 39, 101, 152
The Basement Club pulls in a jovial
mix of expats, locals and travelers
with house music and inexpensive
drinks. Hit the extended happy
hour at the popular Shamrock pub
upstairs before descending into
the subterranean club.

⭐ GLAM *Gay Club*

☎ 4963-2521; www.glambsas.com
.ar; José Antonio Cabrera 3046, Barrio
Norte; 🕒 1am-late Thu-Sat; 🚌 29, 92,
109, 111

One of BA's hottest gay clubs,
Glam comprises three floors,
several bars and lounges, and a
sweaty dance floor that fills with
genetically blessed porteño males.
Come late (3am is ideal) for the
best scenery.

⭐ NOTORIOUS *Jazz Club*

☎ 4813-6888, 4815-8473; www
.notorious.com.ar, in Spanish; Av Callao
966, Recoleta; 🕒 from 9pm; Ⓜ Line D
Callao; ♿

This intimate jazz venue attracts
all ages – devoted locals and curious travelers alike – with nightly
gigs of serious jazz and world
music. Book ahead and visit the
record shop before settling in for
a show.

>PALERMO

Filled with open green spaces where fitness-crazed locals can run and play to their hearts' content, Palermo is a largely residential barrio that separates Recoleta from Palermo Viejo. The neighborhood crawls with stroller-pushing mothers and muscular men racing each other past the rose gardens of sprawling Parque 3 de Febrero (Palermo Woods), a leafy section that also contains the city's botanical gardens, zoo and Japanese gardens, all surrounded by modern high-rise apartment buildings. But there's more to this area than fresh air and middle class comforts. Palermo is home to several embassies and a wealth of museums, from the classic MALBA to the intriguing Evita Museum and the stately Museum of Decorative Arts. Quiet by night, the neighborhood's main thoroughfares, Av Santa Fe and Av del Libertador, buzz during the day with art students on their way to study famous paintings, teenagers typing text messages outside fancy shopping malls, and ambassadors meeting for coffee in elegant glass-fronted cafes.

PALERMO

⦿ SEE

Jardín Botánico
  Carlos Thays 1 A3
Jardín Japonés
  (entrance) 2 C2
Jardín Zoológico 3 B3
La Rural 4 A2
MALBA (Museo de Arte
  Latinoamericano
  de Buenos Aires) 5 D2
Monumento a los
  Españoles 6 B2
Monumento a Sarmiento 7 B2
Museo de Arte Popular
  José Hernández 8 C3
Museo de Artes Plásticas
  Eduardo Sívori 9 A1

Museo Evita 10 B3
Museo Nacional de
  Arte Decorativo 11 D3
Parque 3 de Febrero 12 B1

⌂ SHOP

Alto Palermo 13 C5
Jeans Makers 14 A5
Paseo Alcorta 15 D2

⑪ EAT

Artemisia 16 A6
Lucky Luciano 17 B3
Museo Evita
  Restaurante ....(see 10)

★ PLAY

Bulnes Class 18 B6
Club Aráoz 19 B4
Crobar 20 A1
La Peña del Colorado ...21 B4
Thelonious Club 22 B4

◉ SEE
◉ JARDÍN BOTÁNICO CARLOS THAYS
☎ 4831-4527; Av Santa Fe 3951, Palermo; admission free; 🕙 8am-8pm Nov-Mar & 9am-6pm Apr-Oct; Ⓜ Line D Plaza Italia; ♿

Escape the din of Plaza Italia inside this lush botanical garden, designed by renowned landscape architect Carlos Thays and opened in 1898. It blooms with over 3000 tree and plant species, Roman-style sculptures, floating lily pads on still ponds and an antique iron-and-glass greenhouse originally shown at the 1900 Paris Exhibition.

◉ JARDÍN JAPONÉS
☎ 4804-4922; www.jardinjapones.com, in Spanish; cnr Avs Figueroa Alcorta & Casares, Palermo; admission Mon-Fri $3, Sat & Sun $4; 🕙 10am-6pm; 🚌 10, 37, 67, 102, 130; ♿

Paper lanterns flutter in the breeze, enormous koi fish cluster at the water's edge, tourists snap photos from a footbridge – these are the Japanese gardens, a 1967 gift from the Japanese immigrant community to Buenos Aires. Rare flowers and artificial waterways set an exotic stage for frequent cultural events, yoga classes and tea ceremonies. Stop for sushi in the pagoda-style restaurant.

◉ JARDÍN ZOOLÓGICO
☎ 4011-9900; www.zoobuenosaires .com.ar; cnr Avs Las Heras & Sarmiento, Palermo; adult/under 12yr $13.50/free; 🕙 10am-6pm Tue-Sun; Ⓜ Line D Plaza Italia; ♿

What, you've never heard of a *vicuña*? Even eight-year-old porteños (BA locals) are familiar with this super-skinny camel relative. Expand your knowledge of South American wildlife at the city zoo, which, while overdue for a renovation, houses a host of unusual indigenous animals and kids' favorites like kangaroos and polar bears. The zoo's structures – resembling temples, Roman ruins, and the like – mimic the architecture of the animals' native lands.

LA RURAL
Fashion week, book fairs, farm shows and tango extravaganzas – since 1878, the city's biggest festivals and events have taken place at **La Rural** (☎ 4777-5500; www.larural.com.ar; Plaza Italia). The sprawling urban fairgrounds and convention center, dating to 1878 and conveniently located on Plaza Italia, comprise a series of auditoriums, pavilions and outdoor green spaces. The complex swarms with cattle and cowboys during July's La Rural, the venue's signature livestock show, while intellectual types and art collectors take over the place during annual events like arteBA (p24) and the Feria del Libro (p24).

adventurous temporary exhibits. It also fosters an active film preservation program with a regular schedule of art-house cinema. The design-minded museum shop and cafe are popular with Palermo's art lovers.

◎ MONUMENTO A LOS ESPAÑOLES

cnr Avs del Libertador & Sarmiento, Palermo; Ⓜ Line D Plaza Italia; ◻ 10, 33, 34

This magnificent white monument on broad Av del Libertador was built in 1927. The massive figures at its base represent four regions of Argentina: the Pampas, the Andes, the Chaco and Río de La Plata.

◎ MONUMENTO A SARMIENTO

cnr Avs del Libertador & Sarmiento, Palermo; Ⓜ Line D Plaza Italia; ◻ 10, 33, 34

Rodin crafted this statue of former Argentine president Domingo F Sarmiento, the country's leader from 1868 to 1874 and a key figure in Argentina's education system.

◎ MUSEO DE ARTE POPULAR JOSÉ HERNÁNDEZ

☎ 4803-2384; www.mujose.org.ar, in Spanish; Av del Libertador 2373; admission $3, Sun free; ◷ 1-7pm Wed-Fri, 10am-8pm Sat & Sun; ◻ 10, 37, 59, 60, 92

This small but appealing museum has a permanent collection of

Animals of all sizes live at Jardín Zoológico

◎ MALBA (MUSEO DE ARTE LATINOAMERICANO DE BUENOS AIRES)

☎ 4808-6500; www.malba.org.ar, in Spanish; Av Figueroa Alcorta 3415, Palermo; admission $12, free Wed; ◷ noon-9pm Wed, noon-8pm Thu-Mon; ◻ 17, 67, 124, 130; ♿

Opened in 2001, this landmark contemporary museum houses the Costantini collection of modern Latin American art, along with indigenous Argentine crafts and popular arts, including colorful textiles, decorative masks and Carnaval costumes.

◎ MUSEO DE ARTES PLÁSTICAS EDUARDO SÍVORI

☎ 4774-9452; www.museosivori.org.ar, in Spanish; Parque 3 de Febrero, Av de la Infanta Isabel 555, Palermo; admission $3, free Wed; ☾ noon-6pm Tue-Fri, 10am-6pm Sat & Sun, until 8pm Dec-Jun; 🚌 10, 34; ⛳

Tucked into a quiet corner of Parque 3 de Febrero (Palermo Woods; opposite), this modern art museum shows an outstanding collection of paintings and sculptures by over 100 of Argentina's best artists.

◎ MUSEO EVITA

☎ 4807-9433; www.museoevita.org; Lafinur 2988, Palermo; admission $12; ☾ 1-7pm Tue-Sun; 🚌 15, 59, 60, 64, 93; Ⓜ Line D Plaza Italia ⛳

Whether saint or tyrant (a question posed by the museum's first display), Evita's an icon. The museum dedicated to her life is located in an old building that the first lady's foundation once used as a women's shelter. Check out her glamorous outfits before dining in the courtyard restaurant (p110).

◎ MUSEO NACIONAL DE ARTE DECORATIVO

☎ 4801-8248; www.mnad.org; Av del Libertador 1902, Palermo; admission $3, free Tue; ☾ 2-7pm, closed first 2 weeks of Jan; 🚌 21, 38, 59, 60, 118; ⛳

Housed in an opulent beaux-arts mansion that once belonged to Chilean aristocrats, this museum displays some 4000 pieces of decorative art, from Louis XIV furniture to Renaissance paint-

---

MAD FOR *MATE*

Though Starbucks has officially hit Buenos Aires (the first branch of the megachain opened in 2008 in the Alto Palermo shopping center), you won't see many locals toting styrofoam cups of coffee through the city streets. South Americans are long-time consumers of *mate*, a tea-like drink made by pouring hot water over the leaves of *yerba mate*, a native holly plant. Just as their north-of-the-equator counterparts have portable coffee mugs, Argentines use specific *mate* accoutrements: they pour hot water from a large thermos into a spherical gourd filled with *mate* leaves, then sip the drink through a metal *bombilla* (straw). And porteños drink a *lot* of it – you'll see locals of all ages and economic classes carrying *mate* cases and sipping from gourds at the office, on the street, on picnic blankets and rooftop terraces. *Mate* is an acquired taste, but don't miss the chance to taste it when someone offers – passing around the gourd with friends is a fundamental social ritual.

There are plenty of outdoor activities at Parque 3 de Febrero

ings. The outdoor cafe in the front courtyard is a perfectly quaint setting for a glass of wine.

PARQUE 3 DE FEBRERO
cnr Avs del Libertador & de la Infanta Isabel, Palermo; 🚌 **10, 34, 130;** ♿
Also known as Bosques de Palermo, or Palermo Woods, this sweeping green space abounds with small lakes and paddleboats, pretty gazeboes, stands renting bikes and in-line skates, a monument to literary greats called El Jardín de las Poetas (the Garden of Poets), and the exquisite Rosedal (rose garden.)

Watch your step at night, when Av de la Infanta Isabel becomes a transvestite red-light zone.

🛍 SHOP
🏠 ALTO PALERMO
Shopping Mall
☎ **5777-8000; www.altopalermo.com .ar, in Spanish; Av Coronel Díaz 2098, Palermo;** 🕙 **10am-10pm;** Ⓜ **Line D Bulnes**
Smack on stylish Av Santa Fe, this shiny mall specializes in chic clothing boutiques, jewelry stores, home-decor emporiums – and the city's first Starbucks.

ABASTO & ONCE

The bustling barrios of Abasto and Once, while a little dodgy at night, are part of the 'real' Buenos Aires that's largely unaffected by the tourist trade. Walk west from Congreso along Av Corrientes, or take a quick taxi or Subte ride, to reach this cultural melting pot and commercial district crammed with colorful fabric shops and family-run Jewish and Peruvian eateries. The neighborhood's centerpiece is the historic Mercado de Abasto, previously a massive fresh produce market and now a beautifully restored structure that houses the shopping mall called simply **El Abasto** (☎ 4959-3400; www.abasto-shopping.com.ar, in Spanish; cnr Avs Corrientes & Anchorena; 🕙 10am-10pm; Ⓜ Line B Carlos Gardel). Nearby, on a gentrified street off Av Anchorena is the former home of tango legend Carlos Gardel – now the small but fascinating **Museo Casa Carlos Gardel** (☎ 4964-2071; Jean Jaurés 735; admission $3, free Wed; 🕙 11am-6pm Mon & Wed-Fri, 11am-7pm Sat & Sun; Ⓜ Line B Carlos Gardel). The small tasting cellar at **0800-Vino** (☎ 0800-VINO; www.0800-vino .com, in Spanish; Av Anchorena 695; Ⓜ Line B Carlos Gardel; see also p16) is just a stone's throw from the tango legend's homestead, and one of the city's premiere alternative theater spaces and cultural centers, the bohemian **Ciudad Cultural Konex** (☎ 4864-3200; www .ciudadculturalkonex.org, in Spanish; Av Sarmiento 3131; Ⓜ Line B Carlos Gardel), is housed in a renovated factory a few blocks away.

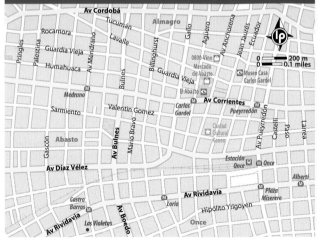

JEANS MAKERS
Fashion

☎ 4865-2420; www.jeansmakers.com;
Soler 4202, Palermo; ⏰ 11am-9pm Mon-
Sat; 🚌 39, 92, 152

Your prayers have been answered.
As the name suggests, Jeans Makers lets you custom-design your
own denims. Get your style down
to a science by combining the
flattering cut of your favorite pair
with cool stitching options and a
range of design detail choices –
and voilà! You've got the jeans of
your dreams.

PASEO ALCORTA
Shopping Mall

☎ 5777-6500; www.paseoalcorta
.com.ar; Salguero 3172, Palermo
Chico; ⏰ 10am-10pm

This upmarket shopping mall
showcases stylish Argentine
brands, exclusive European
designers, a ritzy food court, a
cinema center and a children's
play area.

🍴 EAT

🍴 ARTEMISIA *Vegetarian* $$

☎ 4863-4242; www.artemisiaresto
.com.ar; José Antonio Cabrera 3877, Palermo; ⏰ 8:30pm-late Tue-Sat; 🚌 36,
92, 106; Ⓥ

The homey, vegetarian-friendly
Artemisia is ideal for a low-key
dinner of freshly baked brown
bread, inventive tapas like zucchini bruschetta and mini caprese
skewers, and heart-healthy wok
dishes.

🍴 LUCKY LUCIANO
Italian $$

☎ 4802-1262; Cerviño 3943, Palermo;
⏰ 8:30pm-late Mon-Sat; Ⓜ Line D
Plaza Italia; Ⓥ

It's hard to go wrong with a bowl
of classic spaghetti alla carbonara
and a glass of Cabernet. This Little
Italy-style trattoria is classy but
unpretentious, offering seating in
the garden patio or in the large
dark-wood interior.

SWEET TREATS

With so many foodies analyzing Argentina's beef and waxing poetic about the wine, it's
easy to overlook one of the city's finest epicurean delights – *helado* (ice cream). Thanks to
Argentina's Italian immigrants, most of the ice cream in Buenos Aires is delightfully rich and
available in exotic flavors from *dulce de leche* (a caramel-like local treat) to *maracuya* (passion
fruit). *Heladerías* (ice-cream parlors) offer free samples of their creamy concoctions before you
commit to a flavor (or three). Satiate your sweet tooth properly at a shop displaying the words
elaboración artesanal – this is the real deal, handmade on the premises – or one of the larger
helado franchises around the city.

NEIGHBORHOODS

PALERMO

Taking a rest from the life of Eva Perón at Museo Evita Restaurante

🍴 MUSEO EVITA RESTAURANTE

Modern Argentine   *$$*

☎ 4800-1599; www.museoevita.org; JM Gutierrez 3926, Palermo; 🕙 9am-midnight; Ⓜ Line D Plaza Italia; 🚻 Ⓥ 🚼

Fear not, tourists – though this eatery is located at the Evita museum (p106), it's not a thematic restaurant. The charming tiled courtyard is in fact a picture-perfect spot for lunch, and the cuisine is thoroughly sophisticated. Refined waiters deliver gourmet risotto, pizza and steak to alfresco diners. The first lady's biggest fans prefer to dine inside amid the Evita memorabilia.

⭐ PLAY

⭐ BULNES CLASS *Gay Bar*

☎ 4861-7492; www.bulnesclass.com.ar, in Spanish; Bulnes 1250, Palermo; 🕙 11pm-late Fri & Sat; 🚌 26, 92, 106, 128; 🚼

Bulnes Class attracts a mostly gay crowd to its stylish, minimalist bar. Drop in after dinner but before hitting a club.

⭐ CLUB ARÁOZ *Dance Club*

☎ 4832-9751; www.clubaraoz.com.ar, in Spanish; Aráoz 2424, Palermo; 🕙 1am-late Fri & Sat; 🚌 36, 39, 106, 152

Homesick for hip-hop? Sidestep the city's electrónica scene and head to Club Aráoz to see local break-dancers doing their thing, disco kids throwing back Fernet-and-Coca-Cola cocktails, and music videos illuminating the big screen.

⭐ CROBAR *Dance Club*

☎ 4778-1500; www.crobar.com.ar; Marcelo Freyre s/n, Palermo; 🕙 10pm-late Fri & Sat; 🚌 10, 34, 36

I'VE GOT RESERVATIONS

No one wants to spend precious hours of their vacation waiting in a long queue of hungry, hopeful restaurant patrons. Make sure you're not lost in the dinner crowd by following a few guidelines.

> **Lunch early.** Porteños lunch later, so go at noon to snag a table.
> **Book on weekends.** Reserve ahead of time – and confirm it – on chaotic Friday and Saturday nights.
> **Dinner?** Go early or go late. An empty restaurant isn't appealing, but venues like Gran Bar Danzon (p98) have cocktail bars that draw an earlier crowd. If you don't mind dining late, have a glass of wine at the bar and wait for the night's first sitting to clear out.
> **If you can't book, have a backup plan.** If your heart's set on one restaurant, make sure it's in an area with options – if you can't get in, you'll discover something good (and less hyped) just around the corner.

Nothing beats strong drinks and a supremely attractive crowd of local twenty- and thirty-somethings writhing around on the dance floor. Don't dress to the nines at Crobar – the atmosphere is trendy, but in a laid-back way – and come late on a Friday night for the best scene.

⭐ LA PEÑA DEL COLORADO
Folk Music
☎ 4822-1038; www.delcolorado.com.ar; Güemes 3657, Palermo; admission $25; ⏱ 8pm-late; Ⓜ Line D Bulnes; ♿
This lively spot – which many porteños swear is the best *peña* (folk music venue) in the city – puts on live *folklórica* shows. After the musical set, the performers pass around guitars and country-style

instruments so the happy-go-lucky crowd can get in on the singing and strumming action. Diners can order a set menu ($50) or from the a la carte menu. See also p19.

⭐ THELONIOUS CLUB
Jazz Club
☎ 4829-1562; www.theloniousclub .com.ar; Salguero 1884, Palermo; admission $10-15; ⏱ 9pm-late Wed-Sun; Ⓜ Line D Bulnes; ♿
Get into the jazz mood with a bourbon-infused 'smoky martini' at the bar – or share a bottle of wine in a cozy, darkened booth. The slick, intimate music club features a dynamic agenda of superb live jazz.

>PALERMO VIEJO

Any porteña (BA local) worth her leather clutch purse will tell you that Palermo Viejo is the city's most fashion-forward neighborhood. The heart of the local design and dining scenes bustles by day with stylish young women lugging shopping bags around the designer markets on Plaza Serrano and hipsters clicking through their MacBooks in New York–style delis. By night, the leafy streets throng with beautiful people and serious foodies en route to one of the neighborhood's countless chic eateries and cocktail bars. In case there was any question, the names of Palermo Viejo's subdivisions, Palermo Soho (around Plaza Serrano) and Palermo Hollywood (the hub of BA's film industry, located just across the railroad tracks), clearly reveal the cosmopolitan aspirations of the barrio's trendsetting denizens. This part of town is short on formal sightseeing attractions, but a simple stroll through Palermo Viejo – and its busy designer fairs, petite cobblestoned plazas, low-rise colonial buildings, posh boutiques and sidewalk cafes swarming with voguish locals – provides plenty of cultural stimulation.

PALERMO VIEJO

🏠 SHOP
28 Sport 1 E4
Calma Chicha 2 E4
Cora Groppo 3 E4
DAM 4 E4
Felix 5 E4
Hermanos
  Estebecorena 6 B1
Humawaca 7 E4
Juana de Arco 8 E4
Lo de Joaquin Alberdi ...9 E3
Nadine Zlotogora 10 E4
Papelera Palermo 11 E4
Qara 12 E4
Rapsodia 13 E4

🍴 EAT
Almacén Secreto 14 B5
Azema Exotic Bistró 15 C2

Bar Uriarte 16 D3
Bereber 17 F4
Bio 18 D2
Cluny 19 F4
Don Julio 20 F3
Freud y Fahler 21 E4
Green Bamboo 22 C1
La Dorita 23 D2
Little Rose 24 E4
Miranda 25 C2
Mosoq 26 C2
Ölsen 27 B2
Social Paraíso 28 D4
Standard 29 D1
Sudestada 30 D1

Carnal 33 C3
Casa Cruz 34 D3
Home Hotel 35 B2
Lelé de Troya 36 E3
Malas Artes 37 E5
Mark's Deli 38 E4
Mundo Bizarro 39 D5
Oui Oui 40 C1
Sugar 41 E3

🍸 DRINK
Bangalore Pub & Curry
  House 31 C3
Bar 6 ....32 E4

⭐ PLAY
Bach Bar 42 F5
Kim y Novak 43 F1
La Viruta 44 D5
Los Cardones 45 F3
Niceto Club 46 B3
Salon Canning 47 E5
Sitges 48 F6

Please see over for map

SHOP

28 SPORT
Shoes

☎ 4833-4287; www.28sport.com; Gurruchaga 1481, Palermo Viejo; ⏱ 11am-8pm Mon-Sat; 🚌 93, 142

These funky, two-tone sneakers and boots are affordable and beautifully made with high-quality Argentine leather. The retro shop channels 1950s Americana.

CALMA CHICHA
Fashion, Home Decor

☎ 4831-1818; www.calmachicha.com; Gurruchaga 1580, Palermo Viejo; ⏱ 10am-8pm Mon-Sat, 2-8pm Sun; 🚌 15, 55, 57, 140, 151, 168

The fun, well-priced accessories and home decor at Calma Chicha use Argentine materials to produce items ranging from practical – leather messenger bags and placemats – to kitschy objects like patchwork cowhide throw rugs. A second location is at Honduras 4925.

CORA GROPPO
Women's Fashion

☎ 4833-7474; www.coragroppo.com; cnr El Salvador & Armenia, Palermo Viejo; ⏱ 11am-8pm Mon-Sat; 🚌 15, 39, 55, 168

The talked-about designer behind this sleek high-fashion line is legendary for her reworking of volume and texture in everyday garments. Cora Groppo's striking cropped jackets and multilayered wrap tops make a sophisticated

Stylish accessories (and cowhide throw rugs) abound at Calma Chicha

See Las Cañitas & Belgrano Map p129

Colegiales

Palermo
Hollywood

Braga
Menendez Arte
Contemporaneo

Villa
Crespo

To Casa Felix
(1100m)

Arenal

Dorrego

Arévalo

Dr Emilio Ravignani

Guatemala

Alvarez Thomas

Angel Justiniano Carranza

Bonpland

Gorriti

Honduras

Costa Rica

El Salvador

Humboldt

Nicaragua

Fitz Roy

Soler

Av Juan B Justo

José Antonio Cabrera

Niceto Vega

Av Córdoba

Juan Ramírez de Velasco

Aguirre

Darwin

Av Juan B Justo

Jufre

Castillo

Loyola

Guruchaga

Acevedo

Malabia

Serrano

Guruchaga

Lerma

Scalabrini Ortiz

Uriarte

Camargo

Padilla

40

30
29

6

22

15

26

35

27

25

23

33 31

46

34

16
28

14

39

0   400 m
0   0.2 miles

design statement without over-whelming an ensemble.

🎬 DAM Women's Fashion
☎ 4833-3935; www.damboutique
.com.ar; Honduras 4775, Palermo Viejo;
🕙 11:30am-8:30pm Mon-Sat; 🚌 39,
55, 168

Spice up a boring black wardrobe with a brightly flowered sixties-style dress or a one-piece jump-suit patterned with little green apples from DAM. Playful, vibrant, occasionally outrageous, designer Carola Besasso's casual line is a hit with artistic young porteñas.

🎬 FELIX
Men's Fashion
☎ 4832-2994; www.felixba.com
.ar; Gurruchaga 1670, Palermo Viejo;
🕙 11am-8pm Mon-Sat, 3-8pm Sun;
🚌 15, 39, 55

The spacious, brick-walled Felix stocks casual clothes for fashion-minded college kids and trendy men. You'll see these graphic T-shirts, trench coats, faded jeans, velvet sport jackets, tartan cotton shirts and vintage-inspired sneakers on boys out and about in the barrio.

🎬 HERMANOS ESTEBECORENA
Men's Fashion
☎ 4772-2145; www.hermanosestebe
corena.com; El Salvador 5960, Palermo Hollywood; 🕙 11am-8pm Mon-Sat;
🚌 39, 93, 111

Male urbanites seeking stylish, understated cool have found their mecca at Hermanos Estebecorena. Exquisite tailoring, unusual text-ures and sleek cuts characterize this smart line of slim-cut corduroy trousers, reversible bomber jackets and dapper raincoats.

PERSONAL SHOPPER
Many a fashionista comes to Buenos Aires in pursuit of a particular garment or accessory — calf-skin ankle boots, elbow-length leather gloves, a couture-quality cocktail dress. But navigating the busy local fashion scene can be tricky when you only have a few days to find the object of your design-themed dreams. Let a professional take over: Christina Wiseman of **BAlocal** (☎ 4554-1877; www.balocal.com) runs personalized shopping excursions tailored to a client's taste and price range. Bilingual and well-connected in the city's fashion sphere, Wiseman knows her stuff and, importantly, this chic, energetic ex-New Yorker looks the part. Armed with a file of information about your fashion preferences, she (and a personal driver) will steer you through a selection of boutiques and showrooms. Unusual shopping requests prove Wiseman's know-how: in the past, she's scoured under-the-radar shops and employed local tailors to procure quirky items from an orange crocodile purse to a custom-tailored blue goat-skin reversible jacket.

☐ HUMAWACA *Leather*
☎ 4832-2662; www.humawaca.com; El Salvador 4692, Palermo Viejo; ☼ 11am-8pm Mon-Sat, 2-7pm Sun; 🚌 34, 55, 166
Award-winning designer Ingrid Gutman brings both form and functionality to Argentine leather, producing handbags, backpacks and wallets with clean modernist lines. You'll also see her distinctive collection for sale at MALBA (p105).

☐ JUANA DE ARCO
Women's Fashion
☎ 4833-1621; www.juanadearco.net; El Salvador 4762, Palermo Viejo; ☼ 10am-8pm Mon-Sat; 🚌 34, 39, 55, 166
Designer Mariana Cortés, beloved for her whimsical approach to casual women's fashion, is the creative force behind this exuberant collection of patterned underwear, crocheted swimsuits, conversation-starting woven accessories and animal-stamped pillow cases.

☐ LO DE JOAQUIN ALBERDI
Wine
☎ 4832-5329; www.lodejoaquinalberdi .com.ar; Jorge Luis Borges 1772, Palermo Viejo; ☼ noon-9:30pm; 🚌 34, 39, 55, 168
Argentine wines for every taste and budget line the racks and cellar of this attractive wine shop. Pop across the street to the sister wine-bar, Cabernet, for a glass of Malbec on the patio.

☐ NADINE ZLOTOGORA
Fashion
☎ 4831-4203; www.nadinez.com; El Salvador 4638, Palermo Viejo; ☼ 11am-8pm Mon-Sat; 🚌 15, 39, 55
The quirky, feminine fashions of Nadine Zlotogora exude old-world romance and rustic charm. Recent collections have featured delicate lace and crushed velvet, fitted bodices, long jackets and multilayered skirts. The men's line includes patterned coats and unconventional takes on classic trousers and shirts.

☐ PAPELERA PALERMO
Paper, Gifts
☎ 4833-3081; www.papelerapalermo .com.ar, in Spanish; Honduras 4945, Palermo Viejo; ☼ 10am-8pm Mon-Sat, 2-8pm Sun; 🚌 15, 39, 55, 168
This fashionable paper store is a dream come true for aesthetically minded writers. Stock up on handmade stationery, journals, stamped wrapping paper, stylish address books and beautiful postcards. Cowhide notebooks and tongue-in-cheek Evita photo albums also make unorthodox vacation mementos.

☐ QARA *Leather*
☎ 4834-6361; www.qara.com; Gurruchaga 1548, Palermo Viejo; ☼ 11am-9pm Mon-Sat, 4-8pm Sun; 🚌 39, 55, 168
Moneyed porteñas hit up Qara for chic and thoroughly

contemporary leather bags and accessories. Splurge on an oversized, buttery-soft shoulder bag or pick up something small but smart, like a clutch purse that you can attach to your restaurant table (designed to deter the city's small-time thieves from snatching your keys and wallet).

🏠 RAPSODIA
Women's Fashion

☎ 4832-5363; www.rapsodia.com.ar, in Spanish; El Salvador 4757, Palermo Viejo; 🕐 10am-9pm Mon-Sat, noon-9pm Sun; 🚌 15, 57, 110, 141, 160

According to Rapsodia's designers, this bohemian clothing line was created for women who love music, art and travel. Stop by for flirty skirts, flowing '70s-influenced sundresses and lived-in jeans.

🍴 EAT

🍴 AZEMA EXOTIC BISTRÓ
French, International $$$

☎ 4774-4191; Angel Justiniano Carranza 1875, Palermo Hollywood; 🕐 8am-late Mon-Sat; 🚌 39, 93, 111, 161; 🚹 V

With exotic spices, foreign ingredients and a penchant for crisp white wine, Paul Jean Azema bravely goes where few local chefs have gone before. His eclectic eatery takes inspiration from his diverse travels – tandoori salmon, Vietnamese noodles and tangy ceviche all have their place on the menu – and the simple French-style space is inviting.

🍴 BAR URIARTE
Modern Argentine $$$

☎ 4834-6004; www.baruriarte.com.ar, in Spanish; Uriarte 1572, Palermo Viejo;

CLOSED-DOOR DINING

There's no shortage of fine-dining venues in Palermo Viejo – but as local foodies can attest, overpopulated dining rooms and aloof wait staff can detract from the gastronomic experience. For haute cuisine in a more relaxed setting, check out the *puerta cerrada* (closed door) scene. These intimate eateries, often run out of the chef's home, host just a handful of guests. Fresh seasonal dishes are served in a dinner party-like atmosphere at **Casa Felix** (☎ 4555-1882; www.diegofelix.com; address given with reservation), a *puerta cerrada* that a young Argentine chef and his American wife run out of their quaint Chacarita house. At **Almacén Secreto** (☎ 4775-1271; www.almacensecretoclub.blogspot.com, in Spanish; Aguirre 1242, Villa Crespo), the set-up is less communal – guests order from a short menu of northern Argentine specialties – but the warm, personalized service, quiet courtyard and hidden location on a quiet Villa Crespo side street make you feel like you're having dinner at a friend's house.

Get a nose for modern Argentine food and wine at Bar Uriarte

🕑 noon-4pm & 8pm-1am; 🚌 34, 55, 166; ♿ Ⓥ ♿

This massive, modish space fits Palermo Viejo like a bespoke glove. The front-of-house open kitchen churns out Italian-style pastas and pizzas for trendy local folk. Survey the scene from a couch by the bar, or tuck into the wallet-friendly fixed lunch on the terrace.

🍽 BEREBER
Moroccan $$$
☎ 4833-5662; Armenia 1880, Palermo Viejo; 🕑 8pm-1am Tue-Sun; 🚌 34, 36, 55, 93; Ⓥ

A refreshing slice of the Maghreb, intimate Bereber is scattered with low tables and jewel-toned floor cushions, making it a firm favorite with local couples on a romantic night out. The authentic *pastilla* (meat pie), couscous and tagines sit well with a bottle of red.

🍽 BIO *Vegetarian* $$
☎ 4774-3880; www.biorestaurant.com
.ar, in Spanish; cnr Humboldt & Guatemala, Palermo Hollywood; 🕑 10:30am-5pm Mon, 10:30am-late Tue-Sun; 🚌 9, 11, 93; Ⓥ ♿

So your better half's a devoted carnivore but you're dying for green cuisine? Don't drag them kicking and screaming to an extreme organic eatery, just take them to Bio for fantastically fresh pastas and salads. The homemade ginger lemonade is heavenly.

🍴 CLUNY
Modern European, Argentine $$$

☎ 4831-7176; www.cluny.com.ar, in Spanish; El Salvador 4618, Palermo Viejo; ⏰ noon-4pm & 8:30pm-late Mon-Sat; 🚌 15, 39, 55, 160; ♿

Warm, elegant and stylish, Cluny is a class act. The French-inflected dishes, including duck magret, beef with mustard sauce (divine) and Patagonian lamb with couscous, are beautifully prepared and keep the well-heeled locals coming back.

🍴 DON JULIO *Parrilla* $$

☎ 4831-9564; Cnr Guatemala & Gurruchaga, Palermo Viejo; ⏰ noon-4pm & 8pm-midnight; 🚌 39, 93, 111; ♿ 👶

Classy service and fine wines add an upscale bent to this traditional corner steakhouse. Of course, the *bife de chorizo* (sirloin) is the main attraction at Don Julio, but the exposed-brick interior, dark-wood cutting boards and leather placemats enhance the sensory experience, and the gourmet salads – served with a flourish by the uber-professional wait staff – are a treat.

🍴 FREUD Y FAHLER
Modern Argentine $$

☎ 4833-2153; Gurruchaga 1750, Palermo Viejo; ⏰ noon-3:30pm & 8pm-midnight Mon-Sat; 🚌 39, 55; Ⓥ

Freud y Fahler, despite the name, isn't a high-concept eatery – the cozy, upscale corner spot offers a simple menu of gourmet Mediterranean-inspired and modern Argentine steaks, pastas, risottos and salads. The art gallery crowd often fills the petite space at lunchtime.

🍴 GREEN BAMBOO
Vietnamese $$$

☎ 4775-7050; www.green-bamboo .com.ar, in Spanish; cnr Costa Rica & Angel Justiniana Carranza, Palermo Hollywood; ⏰ 8.30pm-late; 🚌 39, 93, 111, 161; Ⓥ

Retro-Asian and kitschy cool, Green Bamboo is paradise for those craving flavorful Vietnamese cuisine. Reserve ahead – this darkened corner space always gets busy – and start with a signature cocktail made with mint, papaya or passion fruit. Then park yourself in a cushioned corner booth for tongue-searing soups, nutty noodle dishes and savory pork dishes.

🍴 LA DORITA *Parrilla* $$

☎ 4773-0070; cnr Humboldt & Costa Rica, Palermo Hollywood; ⏰ noon-4pm & 8pm-1am; 🚌 21, 111, 161; 👶

Back-to-basics La Dorita grills up well-priced steaks served in a casual atmosphere – televised *fútbol* games indoors, sidewalk tables outdoors. The *parrilla* (grill restaurant) is so popular with locals that it's grown a bigger sibling, La Dorita Enfrente, on the same intersection. Order the house wine and a mini *parrillada* (mixed grill) of three different cuts of beef.

🍴 LITTLE ROSE
Japanese $$

☎ 4833-9496; Armenia 1672, Palermo Viejo; 🕑 12:30-4pm & 8:30pm-12:30am Mon-Sat; 🚌 39, 55, 93

Sashimi and sake are Little Rose's mainstays, but this is no minimalist sushi bar – the sultry candlelit interior is filled with mirrors, shadowy corners and dreamy photographs. Step off the busy shopping street and into this otherworldly little restaurant for a romantic dinner date.

🍴 MIRANDA *Parrilla* $$

☎ 4771-4255; cnr Costa Rica & Fitz Roy, Palermo Hollywood; 🕑 9am-late; 🚌 39, 111, 161

Fashionable Miranda is the *parrilla* of choice for the breed of porteños who crave the classic grilled steaks and *chorizos* they grew up with, but who won't sacrifice style for red meat any day of the week.

🍴 MOSOQ *South American* $$$

☎ 4775-7974; www.mosoq.com, in Spanish; cnr El Salvador & Angel Justiniano Carranza, Palermo Viejo; 🕑 8pm-late Mon-Sat; 🚌 39, 93; 🚻 Ⓥ

Yucca gnocchi, anyone? Sensually lit and visually striking, Mosoq specializes in gourmet Andean cuisine. Adventurous diners come for Peruvian-inspired dishes, while the martini bar draws serious cocktail aficionados to the glittering corner eatery.

🍴 ØLSEN *Scandinavian* $$$

☎ 4776-7677; Gorriti 5870, Palermo Viejo; 🕑 noon-1:30am Tue-Sat, 10:30am-8pm Sun; 🚌 39, 93, 111, 161; 🚻 Ⓥ

With its hip, relaxed vibe, too-cool crowd and dramatic central fireplace, Ølsen could indeed be located in the frosty climes of Scandinavia. The cuisine and service are hit-and-miss, but the vodka selection is superlative. Luxuriate in the garden with a frozen red-berry cocktail – it looks straight out of a magazine – or come for the popular Sunday brunch.

🍴 SOCIAL PARAÍSO
Modern Argentine $$

☎ 4831-4556; www.socialparaiso.com.ar, in Spanish; Honduras 5182, Palermo Hollywood; 🕑 12:30-3:30pm & 8.30pm-midnight Tue-Sat, 12:30-4pm Sun; 🚌 39, 55

One of the originals of the Palermo dining revolution, Social Paraíso is an understated bistro with a short, sophisticated menu that crosses exotic international ingredients with local

COSTANERA NORTE

Dedicated clubbers know BA is firmly positioned on the global clubbing map and will want to hit the clubs along the river on Costanera Norte, a 10-minute taxi ride from Palermo. Most clubs only open on Fridays and Saturdays from around 1am, don't get going until 3am, and don't close until 9am, so take your sunglasses. The best are **Pachá** (☎ 4788-4280; www.pachabuenosaires.com; Av Costanera Rafael Obligado), BA's oldest and best superclub boasting big-name DJs and a riverside terrace; **Rouge** (☎ 4806-8002; Av Costanera Rafael Obligado), big on Friday nights for progressive house with lounges on a waterfront terrace; **Jet** (Av Costanera Rafael Obligado), playing more mainstream sounds; and **Caix** (☎ 4806-9749; Centro Costa Salguero, Av Costanera Rafael Obligado), which starts to heat up around 9am Sunday morning! During summer most clubs move to the coast or to fashionable Punta del Este, Uruguay.

gastronomic staples like steak, fish and Patagonian lamb.

🍴 STANDARD
Modern Argentine $$$

☎ 4779-2774; cnr Guatemala & Fitz Roy, Palermo Hollywood; ⏱ 8pm-late Mon-Sat; 🚌 15, 39, 55, 93

The dark wood paneling, leather chairs and retro bar stools are your first inkling – Standard is a throwback to the 1950s. Get into the mood with a dry martini before perusing the old-fashioned chalkboard menu of gourmet comfort food.

🍴 SUDESTADA
Southeast Asian $$$

☎ 4776-3777; cnr Guatemala & Fitz Roy, Palermo Hollywood; ⏱ noon-3:30pm & 8pm-midnight Mon-Sat; 🚌 15, 39, 55, 93

This minimalist corner space isn't what you'd expect of a Southeast Asian eatery, but Sudestada's curries are the real thing – fiery and flavorful, they'll have you flagging down a waiter for more *agua* in no time. This cool eatery, an institution among local gourmands, offers a welcome change from the steak and potatoes routine.

🍸 DRINK

🍸 BANGALORE PUB & CURRY HOUSE *Bar, Pub*

☎ 4779-2621; Humboldt 1416, Palermo Viejo; ⏱ 6pm-4am; 🚌 39, 152, 168

The spicy Indian sampler platters and juicy burgers at this English-style pub are just as good as the killer pitchers of gin & tonic. Keep company with a nightly horde of youthful locals and expats at Bangalore, run by the same masterminds behind San Telmo's Gibraltar (p80).

▼ BAR 6 *Bar, Cafe*

☎ 4833-6807; www.barseis.com, in Spanish; Armenia 1676, Palermo Viejo; ⏱ 8am-late Mon-Sat; 🚌 15, 39, 160; ♿ 🚹

A stylish neighborhood classic, Bar 6 is open all day – you can drop by for eggs and coffee in the morning or show up at night to lounge on a red velvet couch with a bellini or a beer. The contemporary design, soaring ceilings and foxy crowd make up for the indifferent service.

▼ CARNAL *Bar*

☎ 4772-7582; Niceto Vega 5511, Palermo Viejo; ⏱ 7pm-late Mon-Sat; 🚌 39, 152, 168

See and be seen – preferably in the open air with an icy vodka tonic in hand – on the rooftop terrace at Carnal. A great-looking local crowd shows up every weekend to this ever-popular watering hole.

▼ CASA CRUZ *Bar*

☎ 4833-1112; www.casa-cruz.com; Uriarte 1658, Palermo Viejo; ⏱ 8:30pm-3am; 🚌 34, 55, 166; ♿

This low-lit, drop-dead-gorgeous restaurant is perhaps better known for its happening cocktail bar than for its cuisine (which can be hit-and-miss). Lounge on the lobby's velvet sofas, mojito in hand, to observe a glamorous parade of actresses, athletes and investment bankers entering Casa Cruz through the massive bronze doorway.

▼ HOME HOTEL *Bar*

☎ 4778-1008; www.homebuenosaires .com; Honduras 5860, Palermo Viejo; ⏱ 9:30am-11:30pm; 🚌 39, 93, 111; ♿ 🅥 🚹

This chic, laid-back bar is located inside Home, widely considered the city's coolest and most design-conscious boutique hotel (p136). On warm weekend evenings, DJs spin tunes on the petite poolside patio and the smartly dressed bar staff mix creative drinks.

▼ LELÉ DE TROYA *Bar*

☎ 4832-2726; cnr Costa Rica & Thames, Palermo Viejo; ⏱ noon-late; 🚌 34, 39, 55, 168

One of the barrio's most laid-back bars, Lelé de Troya boasts a summer

Take a break from shopping at Mark's Deli (p124)

terrace that's ideal for kicking back with a glass of white on a warm day.

⛛ MALAS ARTES *Cafe, Bar*
☎ 4831-0743; cnr Honduras & Jorge Luis Borges, Palermo Viejo; ⏱ 8am-late; 🚌 34, 39, 55, 168; ♿
This bohemian corner bar on Plaza Serrano has high ceilings, big picture windows and happy hour specials on beer and cocktails. The sidewalk tables are highly sought after on sunny days.

⛛ MARK'S DELI *Cafe*
☎ 4832-6244; www.markspalermo.com; cnr El Salvador & Armenia, Palermo Viejo; ⏱ 8:30am-9:30pm Mon-Sat, 10:30am-9pm Sun; 🚌 15, 39, 55; ♿ ♿
Cool porteños and bagel-craving travelers pretend like they're in New York at highbrow Mark's Deli, a Manhattan-style cafe that's nearly always packed. If you can score a table, the place is great for cappuccino-and-chocolate-chip cookies while you conduct a post-mortem on your shopping day.

⛛ MUNDO BIZARRO *Bar*
☎ 4773-1967; www.mundobizarrobar .com; Serrano 1222, Palermo Viejo; ⏱ 8pm-3am Sun-Wed, 8pm-4am Thu, 8pm-5am Fri & Sat; 🚌 34, 39, 55, 168
With its vibrant red walls and retro 1950s American diner vibe, Mundo Bizarro has been a Palermo

institution for a decade. This cozy late-night bar draws names from the local music scene and film industry.

⛛ OUI OUI *Cafe*
☎ 4778-9614; Nicaragua 6068, Palermo Viejo; ⏱ 8am-8pm Tue-Fri; 🚌 39, 67, 152; ♿
Pain au chocolat and shabby chic, anyone? Yes please. This immensely popular French-style cafe produces the goods – dark coffee, buttery croissants, jars of tangy lemonade – and boasts a cozy rose-colored interior that's just as charming. Come early to beat the porteña parade.

⛛ SUGAR *Bar*
☎ 15-6894-2002; www.sugarbuenos aires.com; Costa Rica 4619, Palermo Viejo; ⏱ 12:30pm-late Tue-Sat, until 10pm Sun; 🚌 55, 111, 161
This new-on-the-scene expat institution brings in a rowdy crowd with bargain-priced drink specials, comfort food for the homesick and shindigs revolving around political and athletic events – any excuse for a party.

⭐ PLAY
◼ BACH BAR *Lesbian Club*
☎ 15-5877-0919; www.bach-bar.com .ar, in Spanish; José Antonio Cabrera 4390, Palermo; ⏱ 11pm-late Tue-Sun; 🚌 39, 106, 109, 140, 168

Savor French-style coffee and other delights at Oui Oui

This popular lesbian club hosts karaoke nights and raucous live drag shows on weekends.

⭐ KIM Y NOVAK *Bar, Club*

☎ 4773-7521; cnr Güemes & Godoy Cruz, Palermo; ⏰ 9:30pm-late Tue-Sun; 🚌 34, 55, 93; Ⓜ Line D Plaza Italia

Technically, Kim y Novak is a bar, not a club – but the wild transvestite and hipster crowd baring flesh and downing cocktails to a DJ-spun soundtrack make this grungy, flamboyant corner venue an underground nightlife staple. Gay, straight, the guy with pink

hair and nipple rings – everyone is welcome at the one-of-a-kind Kim y Novak.

⭐ LA VIRUTA *Tango*

☎ 4774-6357; www.lavirutatango.com; Armenia 1366, Palermo Viejo; ⏰ class times vary, *milonga* midnight Fri-Sun; 🚌 15, 55, 168

This colorful midnight *milonga*, happening in the humble basement of the Armenian community center, sees dancers of all ages crowding the floor. La Viruta is friendly and atmospheric, a mustsee for tango enthusiasts. See p138.

Luciana Messina
Flight attendant and textile design student

How does Buenos Aires compare to other world capitals? This isn't New York or London, but it's one of the most cosmopolitan cities in Latin America We have a lot in common with Italians – porteños can be superficial and critical, but we're also warm and funny. **Which local designers do you admire?** Pablo Ramírez (p75), and Hermanos Estebecorena (p116) for menswear. **Best place to meet a friend for coffee?** Oui Oui (p124). It's cozy and French, with local elements, like the *dulce de leche* cakes and mismatched cutlery. **Best da spot?** Little Rose (p121) is beautiful. **And for after-dinner cocktails?** Mundo Bizarro (p124) has excellent bartenders and creative drinks, it's a cool place. **Any tips for travelers?** Come to Buenos Aires on a weekend. Head to Palern for art galleries, MALBA (p105), designer boutiques and restaurants. Don't m. Recoleta cemetery (p93) or the design market on Plaza Francia (p96).

⭐ LOS CARDONES *Peña*

☎ 4777-1112; www.cardones.com.ar, in Spanish; Jorge Luis Borges 2180, Palermo Viejo; 🕐 from 8.30pm Wed-Sat; 🚌 34, 36, 55, 93; Ⓜ Line D Plaza Italia

A cheap and cheerful *peña* (folk-music venue) alive with regional music and free-flowing wine, Los Cardones is a welcome change of pace from the barrio's posturing cocktail bars and clubs. See also p19 for more info.

⭐ NICETO CLUB
Dance Club, Concert Venue

☎ 4779-9396; www.nicetoclub.com, in Spanish; Niceto Vega 5510, Palermo Viejo; 🕐 from 1am Thu-Sat; 🚌 21, 93, 111, 151, 168

Niceto's huge popularity rests on its all-inclusive structure – divided into two venues, the club brings in both an outrageously dressed gay-straight crowd for the hedonistic Club 69 party and legions of urban hipsters for the famed Zizek electronic nights. Come for cutting-edge music from rock to reggae, cheap drinks and *buena onda* (good vibes).

⭐ SALON CANNING *Tango*

☎ 4832-6753; Av Scalabrini Ortiz 1331, Palermo Viejo; 🕐 classes 7-11pm Mon, Tue & Fri, 9-11pm Thu, *milonga* 11pm-4am Mon-Fri; 🚌 15, 29, 39, 57, 168

Salon Canning attracts a young, local crowd of *tangueros* to a variety of *milongas*. The place gets especially busy on Monday and Tuesday nights when tango DJs hit the turntables for the dynamic Parakultural event. See the website for details: www.parakultural.com.ar.

⭐ SITGES *Gay Club*

☎ 4861-3763; www.sitgesonline.com.ar; Av Córdoba 4119, Palermo; 🕐 10.30pm-late Wed-Sun; 🚌 92, 140, 168

This spacious brick-walled club, illuminated by funky chandeliers and a blue-glowing bar, gets hectic on weekends when gay and lesbian partygoers drop by before heading to Glam (p101). Catch the amusing drag show on Wednesday nights.

>LAS CAÑITAS & BELGRANO

On either side of Av del Libertador in the far north of the city are two neighborhoods that are close together on the map, but far apart in character. Las Cañitas is a trendy pocket of Palermo where the city's pretty young things drink and dance, while Belgrano, a green suburb-like barrio where porteño (BA local) families migrate when they need more space for the *niños* (children) to play, feels like BA's version of Brooklyn. Head to Belgrano to shop around the main thoroughfare, Av Cabildo, before stopping for tea in BA's tiny Chinatown. Save a trip to Las Cañitas for a day at the races – the city's polo grounds and horse racetrack border the neighborhood on the south side – or for a night on the town. Past the expensive loft-style apartments and fitness centers of Las Cañitas, Av Báez runs through a few dense blocks of fashionable sushi bars and rollicking pubs where rich local kids spill out onto the sidewalk, Coronas in hand, on balmy nights.

LAS CAÑITAS & BELGRANO

◉ SEE
Barrio Chino 1 B1
Museo de Arte
　Español 2 A1

⌂ SHOP
Anuva Vinos 3 D3
Ashes of Roses 4 E3
Corre Lola 5 A2
Fundación Silataj 6 A2
Valenti 7 A2

⍾ EAT
Cantina Chinatown 8 B1
Lotus Neo Thai 9 B1
Moshi Moshi 10 E3
Novecento 11 E4

▼ DRINK
Kandi 12 E3
Pipí-Cucú 13 C4
Soul Café &
　Supersoul 14 E4
Van Koning 15 E3

★ PLAY
Campo Argentino
　de Polo 16 F3
Hipódromo
　Argentino 17 F3

SEE

BARRIO CHINO

cnr Arribeños & Mendoza, Belgrano;
Ⓜ Line D Juramento; ♿
BA's petite but exuberant Barrio
Chino (Chinatown), established by
Taiwanese immigrants after WWII,
is worth a visit for the great-value
noodle and spring roll joints and
exotic supermarkets where you
can gawk at beheaded fish and
pick up treats like lychee candy
and beautifully packaged sake.

MUSEO DE ARTE ESPAÑOL

☎ 4783-2640; www.museolarreta
.buenosaires.gov.ar, in Spanish;
Juramento 2291, Belgrano; admission $1,
free Thu ☼ 2-8pm Mon-Fri, 10am-8pm
Sat & Sun; Ⓜ Line D Juramento
Once the colonial home of modernist writer Enrique Larreta, the
Museo de Arte Español (Museum
of Spanish Art) now shows the
author's personal collection of
contemporary Spanish artwork.

SHOP

ANUVA VINOS Wine

☎ 15-6858-4759; www.anuvawines
.com; Av Luis Maria Campos 545, Las
Cañitas; ☼ 10am-7pm Mon-Fri; 🚌 15,
29, 55
The business headquarters of Anuva Vinos, an upscale American-run
wine club that conducts tastings
at venues around town (see p16).

ASHES OF ROSES
Women's Fashion

☎ 4772-5144; www.ashesofroses.com
.ar, in Spanish; Argüibel 2874, Las Cañitas;
☼ 10am-8pm Mon-Fri; 🚌 15, 29, 55
Romantic, vintage-inspired
dresses, diaphanous sweaters and
uber-feminine floral accessories
line the racks at this lovely Cañitas
boutique.

CORRE LOLA Shoes

☎ 4780-0553; www.correlola.com.ar,
in Spanish; Mendoza 2493, Belgrano;
☼ 10am-8pm Mon-Fri; Ⓜ Line D
Juramento
This whimsical footwear line features ballerina flats in every color
of the rainbow, knee-high boots
in patent leather, cork wedge plat-
forms with oversized flower appli-
qués and leather sandals in candy
shades of jade and magenta.

FUNDACIÓN SILATAJ
Souvenirs, Handicrafts

☎ 4785-8371; www.fundacionsilataj
.org.ar; Vuelta de Obligado 1933, Belgrano;
☼ 9:30am-1pm & 3:30-8pm Mon-Fri,
9:30am-1pm Sat; Ⓜ Line D Juramento
The hand-woven woolen mittens
go for 30 pesos, but the fair-trade
opportunity, as they say, is price-
less. Fundación Silataj supports
the indigenous artisans of northern Argentina. Go on a responsible
shopping spree and pick up some
gorgeous wooden serving dishes.

You'll find something wild to take home at Fundación Silataj

VALENTI Wine, Deli

☎ 4783-0324; www.valenti.com.ar;
Vuelta de Obligado 1820, Belgrano;
🕒 9am-9pm Mon-Sat & 10am-2pm Sun;
Ⓜ Line D José Hernández

All the fixings for a gourmet picnic
are on mouthwatering display
here – exotic cheeses, cured
Patagonian meats, pâté and wine
sourced from small bodegas.

EAT
MOSHI MOSHI

Sushi $$$

☎ 4772-2005; www.moshi-moshi.com
.ar, in Spanish; cnr Ortega y Gasset &
Soldado de la Independencia 1707, Las
Cañitas; 🕒 8:30pm-late Tue-Sun; 🚌 15,
29, 55, 60, 64

Like the tasteful loft apartments
that line the block, this posh 1st-
floor Japanese restaurant is outfit-
ted in white minimalist decor. The
discerning (and calorie-counting)
Cañitas set comes here for fresh
takes on tempura and noodles.

NOVECENTO

International $$$

☎ 4778-1900; www.bistronovecento
.com; cnr Av Báez & Argüibel, Las Cañitas;
🕒 noon-4pm & 8pm-late; 🚌 15, 29,
55, 60, 64

Grilled steak, suckling pig, Asian-
style stir-fry or an American-style
breakfast with eggs and coffee –
this smart, good-looking bistro offers an eclectic menu (and actually
pulls it off).

LAS CAÑITAS & BELGRANO

WHAT'S YOUR BEEF?

Your mouth waters, your pulse races, your mind reels: it must be your first time standing near the countless cuts of steak sizzling on the *parrilla* (grill). Easy there – the local carnivore culture isn't so complex when you learn the basics. Argentina's definitive steak is the *bife de chorizo* (sirloin; not to be confused with the sausage called simply *chorizo*). Other popular cuts include *bife de lomo* (tenderloin), the succulent *ojo de bife* (rib eye) and *bife ancho* (a boneless rib cut). *Churrasco*, a thin steak, is a favorite quick-fix meal for gauchos. Porteños like their beef cooked through, so if you like your steak a little juicier, ask for *jugoso* (rare) or *a punto* (medium-rare). Try adding some extra flavor to the meat with a dash of *chimichurri* (oil and herb sauce) and – need it be said? – be sure to wash down your red meat with a fine red wine.

⅄ DRINK

⅄ KANDI *Bar, Club*
☎ 4772-2453; Av Báez 340, Las Cañitas; ⏲ 8pm-late; 🚌 15, 29, 59, 60, 64; ♿

This retro cocktail bar, with its caramel leather seating, round mirrors and wooden floors, is cool, design-wise, and a hit with the local hipsters who pile in after midnight.

⅄ PIPÍ-CUCÚ *Bar, Club*
☎ 4551-9314; Ciudad de la Paz 557, Belgrano; ⏲ 10am-1am Mon-Sat; 🚌 42, 59, 152; ♿

No, it's not a Native American tribal name – Pipí-Cucú is a local expression meaning 'gorgeous.' This artistic cocktail bar and brasserie is fashionable and coolly understated – everything from the chairs to the wine glasses are mismatched.

⅄ SOUL CAFÉ & SUPERSOUL
Bar, Club
☎ 4778-3115; Av Báez 245/252, Las Cañitas; ⏲ 8pm-late Tue-Sun; 🚌 15, 29, 59, 60, 64; ♿

These 1970s-style sister bars are equally groovy. Fun-loving Soul Café is furnished with kitschy hanging dice lamps and stylish white seats, while Supersoul has curvy red walls, hanging disc 'curtains' and a long wall mirror that makes people-watching (and full-out ogling) possible.

⅄ VAN KONING *Bar*
☎ 4772-9909; Av Báez 325, Las Cañitas; ⏲ 7pm-late; 🚌 15, 29, 59, 60, 64; ♿

When the barrio's generically stylish bars leave you longing for something more, head to this Dutch-style pub. Rustic dark-wood booths, candlelight and frosty pints of Otro Mundo (a local micro-brew), draw a lighthearted crowd.

NOODLES & TEA

Buenos Aires' little Chinatown is the barrio to be in when you feel like trading your steak knife for a pair of *palitos* (chopsticks). Fried-rice-and-jasmine-tea purists favor traditional, family-run diners like the cheerful **Cantina Chinatown** (☎ 4783-4173; Cnr Arribeños & Mendoza; ☽ noon-3:30pm & 8pm-midnight Mon-Sat.) Plop down at a table by the corner window and order up tender *empanadas chinas a la plancha* (pot-stickers) and a deep, steaming bowl of rice noodle soup seasoned with delicious Argentina beef. Style-conscious types opt to dine at a more contemporary eatery like **Lotus Neo Thai** (☎ 15-6628-0529; www.restaurante lotus.com.ar, in Spanish; Arribeños 2265; ☽ 8pm-late Mon-Sat), a Las Cañitas institution that recently made the move to Barrio Chino. Kick back with the heady, mint-infused house cocktail at this blissful Thai eatery where painted lotus flowers climb the walls and guests recline on floor cushions. The duck curry and pad thai, when requested, pack heat.

⭐ PLAY

⭐ CAMPO ARGENTINO DE POLO DE PALERMO *Sport*

☎ 4777-6444; www.aapolo.com, in Spanish; cnr Avs del Libertador 4300 & Dorrego, Las Cañitas; admission $15-60; 🚍 15, 29, 55, 60, 64; ⑤

Argentina is deservedly famous for polo. A springtime match is more than a display of athletic prowess – it's a chance to watch BA's upper crust in action. The players' expensive haircuts and spiffy uniforms render them almost as elegant as the horses they rode in on.

⭐ HIPÓDROMO ARGENTINO *Sport*

☎ 4778-2800; www.palermo.com.ar, in Spanish; cnr Avs del Libertador 4101 & Dorrego, Las Cañitas; admission $5-10; ☽ Sat-Mon; 🚍 10, 37, 160; ⑤

Even if you're not usually a fan, a few hours at the horseraces in the glamorous grandstand of the historic Hipódromo Argentino is a fabulous afternoon outing (with first-rate people-watching, to boot). The big race of the season is the Gran Premio Nacional in November.

Buenos Aires is a vibrant metropolis crowded with architectural monuments, contemporary art galleries, tango halls, fashionable boutiques, traditional steakhouses, open-air antique markets, atmospheric old cafes, leather shops, stylish cocktail bars and lively nightclubs. Read up on the basics to expand your savoir faire before diving into the urban fray.

> Accommodations	136
> Tango	138
> Music	140
> Food	141
> Bars	142
> Clubs	143
> Gay & Lesbian BA	144
> Fashion	145
> Estancias	146
> Art	147
> Sports	148
> Architecture	149
> Buenos Aires with Kids	150

Floralis Genérica (p94) opens its metallic petals heavenward, Recoleta

ACCOMMODATIONS

Prices are slowly but surely rising in Buenos Aires, and while steak and wine still seem like a steal to foreigners, nightly hotel rates are approaching those of any world capital. Still, you don't have to break the bank for a chance to fall asleep to the melancholy strains of tango music. Many of the city's smaller boutique hotels and guesthouses are both charming and fairly priced, while several of the grander hotels offer frequent web deals and weekend packages – and true budget travelers take their pick from a wide range of hostels competing for business by offering rooftop *asados* (barbecues) and wi-fi. Review your options before setting foot on Argentine soil to allow yourself the best possible range of options.

At the top of the accommodation food chain are the opulent Louis XIV-style **Alvear Palace Hotel** (www.alvearpalace.com) and the luxe **Palacio Duhau-Park Hyatt** (www.buenosaires.park.hyatt.com), both standing grandly on Recoleta's ritzy Av Alvear. Their gorgeous marble spas and white-gloved afternoon tea service ensure a first-class experience for visiting socialites and dignitaries. Rock stars and fashion models with pesos to spare usually opt instead for the **Faena Hotel + Universe** (www.faenahotelanduniverse.com), the sultry Philippe Starck–designed paradise in Puerto Madero.

Further down the chain are some of the city's most stylish sleeps – the cool contemporary boutique hotels of Palermo Viejo. Award-winning **Home Hotel** (www.homebuenosaires.com), thanks to a sleek pool bar and cutting-edge interior design, is usually booked far in advance. Newer boutique hotels like **Vitrum** (www.vitrumhotel.com) and **Legado Mítico** (www.legadomitico.com) also draw a fashionable clientele who want to sleep in the vicinity of Palermo's happening art, fashion, and dining scene.

 Hotels & Hostels

Need a place to stay? Find and book it at lonelyplanet.com. Over 60 properties are featured for Buenos Aires – each personally visited, thoroughly reviewed and happily recommended by a Lonely Planet author. From hostels to high-end hotels, we've hunted out the places that will bring you unique and special experiences. Read independent reviews by authors and other travelers, and get practical information including amenities, maps and photos. Then reserve your room simply and securely via Hotels & Hostels – our online booking service. It's all at lonelyplanet.com/hotels.

Shorter on design amenities but long on local character are the bohemian guesthouses and small hotels of San Telmo, like the lovely tango-themed **Mansíon Dandi Royal** (www.mansiondandiroyal.com) and the petite colonial-style **Posada Luna** (www.posadaluna.com). Ideally positioned for sightseeing in the Microcentro, Retiro, Puerto Madero and La Boca, San Telmo's accommodations are housed in historic buildings and situated nearby neighborhood *parrillas* (grill restaurants) and cafes.

Innumerable midrange hotels are scattered across the city, offering standard accommodations and myriad mod cons to business travelers and families; apartment-style hotels like **Art Suites** (www.artsuites.com.ar) are great value. Similarly widespread are Buenos Aires' various hostels, offering communal space and some private rooms to young travelers and backpackers. Try **Casa Jardín** (www.casajardinba.com.ar) in Palermo Viejo or, on the south side of the city, San Telmo's cool **Ostinatto** (www.ostinatto.com).

Hotel staff throughout Buenos Aires are usually happy to help you arrange Spanish classes or book a tango show – just ask. No matter where you stay, taxis are cheap, plentiful and fast. Usually it takes no more than 20 minutes and costs around $20 to travel from Palermo to San Telmo – the Subte, depending on traffic, is often even faster.

MOST UNIQUE SLEEPS
> Faena Hotel + Universe (www.faena hotelanduniverse.com)
> Mansíon Dandi Royal (www.mansion dandiroyal.com)
> Legado Mítico (www.legadomitico.com)
> Esplendor de Buenos Aires (www .esplendorbuenosaires.com)

BEST BOUTIQUE HOTELS
> Home Hotel (www.homebuenosaires .com)
> Tailor Made Hotel (www.tailormade hotels.com.ar)
> Five Cool Rooms (www.fivebuenos aires.com)
> 1555 Malabia House (www.malabia house.com.ar)
> Bo Bo Hotel (www.bobohotel.com)

MOST BANG FOR YOUR BUCK
> Casa Alfaro (www.casaalfaro.com.ar)
> The Four Hotel (www.thefourhotel .com.ar)
> Posada de la Luna (www.posadaluna .com)
> Che Lulu Trendy Hotel (www.luluguest house.com)
> La Otra Orilla (www.otraorilla.com.ar)

BEST FOR DESIGN GEEKS
> Moreno 376 (www.morenobueno saires.com)
> Vitrum (www.vitrumhotel.com)
> cE Design (www.designce.com)
> 248 Finisterra (www.248finisterra .com)
> Craft Hip Hotel (www.crafthotel.com)

TANGO

Some days at sunset, the whole of Buenos Aires seems to be moving to the rhythm of a tango soundtrack – old gents deal cards in corner bars while Carlos Gardel's voice wafts out of a transistor radio, a child plays the *bandoneón* (accordion) for tourists on the Subte, and local dancers warm up for a nightly *milonga* (social dance) as the beat-up sound system plays tango classics. The iconic dance and musical form are experiencing a revival in Buenos Aires. Not only do the nostalgic old tango dancers have a renewed sense of pride in the tradition, foreigners are doubly entranced by the melancholic tango. Walk past the Sunday night *milonga* in San Telmo's Plaza Dorrego (p73) and you'll see eager young travelers putting their first tango lessons to the test, dancing cheek-to-cheek with distinguished-looking partners three times their age. Social dances in tango dance halls are particularly popular, and while the afternoon *milonga* at Confitería Ideal (p45; pictured right) attracts a sizable crowd, the Saturday night *milonga* (which runs until 4am) is packed.

For many years, tango was despised by the porteño (BA local) elite and considered a vulgar pastime of the working class. The dance had humble beginnings, to be sure. It got going at the end of the 19th century in Buenos Aires' brothels, where a melting pot of poor immigrants and country folk danced together while waiting their turn to slip behind the bedroom door. The tango drew on stylistic influences from African, Spanish, Italian and traditional Argentine dance forms. Developed by men who had left their families behind to start a life in Argentina's bustling capital city, the dance expressed machismo, passion, longing and a fighting edge – and was set to an emerging sound rooted in Spanish and Italian melodies, *criollo* (Argentine-born) verse and Afro-Uruguayan *candombe* (a drum-based rhythm).

When Argentine musicians took tango to Paris at the beginning of the 20th century, it quickly swept through the ballrooms of Europe. By 1913, everyone wanted to dance the tango, and only then did the porteño aristocrats embrace the trend in the upscale dance halls of Recoleta. In 1917, Carlos Gardel (see the boxed text, p56) recorded the poetic 'Mi Noche Triste' (My Sad Night). Considered the genre's first anthem, it featured Gardel's crooning, charismatic voice and set a new standard – laments of lost love, faraway mothers and changing barrios would become the musical expression of the porteño psyche.

The genre continued to transform throughout the following decades with the introduction (and later decline) of orchestras. By the 1970s, the legendary Astor Piazzolla, a master on the *bandoneón*, was moving tango out of the dance halls and blending the form with jazz and classical music in international music venues. After the economic crisis of 2001, former rocker Daniel Melingo experimented with adding a harder edge to tango and trading the old-fashioned text for contemporary lyrics. Music collectives Bajofondo Tango Club (now known simply as Bajofondo) and Paris-based Gotan Project ignited tango electrónica, an energetic and sensual music form that's become extremely popular in Buenos Aires and abroad.

If tango tops your must-do list, start by seeing a tango show or stopping by a *milonga*. Private and group lessons are available in dance halls and advertised throughout the city. For more information on tango travel, packages, tours, shows, lessons and *milongas*, check out the following websites: www.tangodata.com.ar (the official Argentine government tango portal); www.buenosairesmilongas.com (comprehensive listing of local *milongas*); and www.argentinatango.com, www.tangoafficionado.com and www.triptotango.com (informative foreign sites offering tango package tours and listing BA *milonga* venues).

BEST TANGO SHOWS
> El Querandí (p83)
> El Viejo Almacén (p83)
> Bar Sur (p82)
> 36 Billares (p59)
> La Cumparsita (p83)

BEST MILONGAS
> Confitería Ideal (p45)
> Salon Canning (p127)
> El Beso (p60)
> Centro Region Leonesa (p61)
> La Viruta (p125)

MUSIC

Buenos Aires is alive with the sound of music – with melancholy tango melodies, yes, but also with lively *rock nacional* (Argentine rock), seductive tango electrónica, operatic arias, DJ-spun *cumbia* (Colombian-born beats popularized in the slums of BA) and folk music from the north like the *chamamé* and *chacarera*. Whether you'd prefer to kick back at a jazz club or listen to guitar-strumming gauchos, don't miss a nighttime sojourn into Buenos Aires' colorful music scene.

The nation's great unifying force could well be *rock nacional*, a mainstream rock-and-roll genre – porteño mechanics and businessmen alike know the words to hits produced by Charly García and his trailblazing '70s group Sui Generis. The uber-popular 1980s outfit Soda Stereo paved the way for today's headliners, from rock groups like Divididos and Fito Páez to the clever folk-pop troubadour Kevin Johansen.

Rock nacional songwriters who experimented with ethnic forms heralded the popular revival of Argentine *folklórica* (folk music). This evocative blend of traditional Andean music and European rhythms, pioneered by the masterful Mercedes Sosa, is performed nightly at *peñas* (folk venues) across the city.

The city's grand theaters provide glamorous settings for the flourishing classical music scene, while jazz is on at smoky subterranean bars and a string of nightclubs host innovative DJs spinning Latin gangster beats for the younger set. Tango fans can hear *orquestas típicas* (tango orchestras) performing in *milongas* – or have a listen to something fresher, the dramatic tango electrónica. See the agenda at www.whatsupbuenos aires.com for music listings.

BEST FOR A LITTLE NIGHT MUSIC

> Thelonious Club (p111)
> Los Cardones (p127)
> La Peña del Colorado (p111)
> Notorious (p101; pictured right)
> Centro Cultural Torquato Tasso (p82)

FOOD

Little more than a decade ago, basic steak, pasta and pizza were the extent of Argentine cuisine – but recently, the city's gastronomic horizons have widened considerably. A well-traveled generation of savvy restaurateurs and talented chefs have brought their newfound know-how to the dinner table, offering fresh takes on classic Argentine dishes. Factor in the supreme quality of Argentina's meat and produce (and the still-favorable exchange rate for many tourists) and voilà! You're in foodie heaven.

Many of the city's most stylish and adventurous restaurants are in Palermo Viejo. The barrio's cobblestoned streets are mobbed at night by well-dressed porteños sharing tapas at sidewalk tables and parading into bustling brasseries, seductively lit Thai eateries, and high-class sushi bars. A few upmarket *parrillas* also draw a discerning local crowd, though your best bet for steak with local character is further south in the San Telmo barrio. These classic restaurants could often use a lick of paint – you won't find polished concrete floors or mood music here – but these inexpensive old-time eateries feed the city's soul with brilliant beef fresh from the grill (see p22). The perfect accompaniment to this carnivore's delight is, of course, an outstanding Argentine Malbec (see p16).

The only downside for jetlagged visitors is that porteños eat late. Restaurants rarely open for dinner before 8pm, and tables don't start filling up until after 10pm. Dinner is a leisurely affair, so you'll get to bed late and rise as the locals do with a breakfast of *medialunas* (pastries) and coffee.

BEST STEAK DINNER
> Don Julio (p120)
> La Brigada (p77; pictured right)
> La Dorita (p120)
> Miranda (p121)
> Gran Parrilla del Plata (p77)

BEST CONTEMPORARY CUISINE
> 788 Food Bar (p98)
> La Vinería de Gualterio Bolívar (p77)
> Mosoq (p121)
> Café San Juan (p76)
> Green Bamboo (p120)

BARS

Porteños love to get dolled up and hit the town, but you won't see any locals getting plastered at the corner bar. The natives don't imbibe much compared with Europeans and North Americans – maintaining composure is a point of pride – so it stands to reason when they go out for a drink (that's right, one drink), they don't bother with cheap beer or shots of vodka. Locals generally opt for microbrews, cocktails made with fresh fruit juice, or a glass of Malbec when they meet friends for happy hour or late-night drinks on the weekend. On weekdays, the bar scene gets going after work as young businessmen loosen their ties at wine bars like Gran Bar Danzon (p98) and a casual bohemian set goes for beers and *picadas* (cheeses, meats and olives served on a wooden breadboard) at low-key watering holes like Dadá (p69) or El Federal (p80). After dinner, cool and moody venues like La Cigale (p43; pictured below) and Mundo Bizarro (p124) see a round of hand-holding couples and groups of friends. The spirits start flowing much later on Friday and Saturday nights – many venues are still near-empty at midnight – when locals bar-hop through the open-air terraces and intimate lounges of Palermo Viejo. The fashionable barrio, home to hot spots like Carnal (p123), Bar 6 (p123) and Casa Cruz (p123), hums with nightlife; many of the city's most talented bartenders mix their inventive concoctions here for a mellow, good-looking crowd. The locals certainly aren't afraid to burn the candle on both ends – unless you're a night owl, you probably won't be around for the last call.

BEST FOR LAID-BACK DRINKS
> Dadá (p69)
> Bar Seddón (p79)
> Pipí-Cucú (p132)
> Van Koning (p132)
> La Cigale (p43)

BEST FOR EXOTIC COCKTAILS
> Milión (p99)
> 647 (p79)
> Le Bar (p44)
> Casa Cruz (p123)
> Ølsen (p121)

CLUBS

With a reputation for long nights and early mornings, Buenos Aires has always had a thumping club scene. When house music took the world by storm in the late 1980s, followed by techno in the '90s, dance clubs opened all over the city, including an outpost of legendary Pachá (p122; pictured below). Porteño Hernán Cattaneo became Pachá's resident DJ in 1996, and was soon spinning alongside big names such as Paul Oakenfold, John Digweed, Dave Seaman and Sasha. Now Cattaneo is one of the world's hottest DJs, and porteños nod with approval when they see posters plastered on walls promoting dance parties he's headlining.

As a general rule, Buenos Aires' clubs don't open their doors before midnight, and most porteños don't start lining up until 2am. Most clubs don't close until morning, usually between 7am and 9am, so bring some sunglasses for the next day. Take small notes for taxis too (never hand over a $100 note), as clubs are scattered around the city. Entry fees range from $5 to $30, though prices run a lot higher for major dance events. Serious clubbers should focus their energies on Costanera Norte clubs (p122), while those looking to get home before the sun comes up should check out more laid-back venues like El Living (p59) or the Basement Club (p101).

Check out www.surfacebookings.com.ar for DJ tours and dance events and links; and www.buenosaliens.com for comprehensive links and listings of DJs, clubs, events, music companies and DJ gear.

BEST UP-ALL-NIGHT CLUBS
> Crobar (p110)
> Niceto Club (p127)
> Cocoliche (p45)
> Club Aráoz (p110)
> Pachá (p122)

BEST FOR A FEW HOURS ON THE TOWN
> Museum (p83)
> El Living (p59)
> Basement Club (p101)
> Asia de Cuba (p51)
> Maluco Beleza (p60)

GAY & LESBIAN BA

Progressive Buenos Aires is one of Latin America's gay capitals and a city that's open to alternative lifestyles (what else would you expect of a culture built on tango, a sensual dance originally performed by a pair of men?). Argentina, after all, has recognized same-sex civil unions since 2003, and for World AIDS Day 2005 it boldly dressed its beloved Obelisco (p40) in a bright pink condom.

The queer scene ranges from establishments that are simply billed as 'gay-friendly' but attract a mixed clientele – like mellow Pride Café (p82) and **Palermo Viejo B&B** (www.palermoviejobb.com) – to heaving clubs complete with dancing boys and dark rooms, like Glam (p101), and South America's first five-star gay hotel, the flamboyant **Axel** (www.axelhotels.com). By comparison to the happening all-boys scene, the lesbian domain is quieter and more covert, but you'll find a high concentration of gay women at smaller hot spots like Bach Bar (p124).

Though Buenos Aires' thriving gay scene has been compared to that of San Francisco, there's no barrio here that's equivalent to the Castro – the local queer sphere is spread across San Telmo, Retiro, Barrio Norte and Palermo Viejo. Navigate the rainbow flag-waving scene through a gay travel agency like **Pride Travel** (www.pride-travel.com) or **Step Gay** (www.stepgay.com). Pick up the excellent *Gay Map* (an interactive version is at www.gaymaps .org), available for free in bars and hotels and highlighting gay-friendly restaurants, bars, cinemas, spas and shops.

BEST GAY-FRIENDLY EATERIES
> Pride Café (p82)
> Empire Thai (p67)
> Cluny (p120)

BEST GAY & LESBIAN CLUBS
> Club 69, Niceto Club (p127)
> Bulnes Class (p110)
> Glam (p101)
> Sitges (p127)

FASHION

Buenos Aires is overrun with high-fashion boutiques and multibrand showrooms where the racks are crammed with designs by up-and-coming trendsetters. Prices have risen in recent years, but the city's still a shopper's playground rife with fashionable and (relatively) affordable trench coats, avant-garde cocktail dresses, slim-cut wool sweaters and leather boots that will inspire your friends back home to book a plane ticket to Argentina faster than the salesgirl can say 'Visa or Mastercard?'

Palermo Soho is the beating heart of the city's high fashion scene and home to the flagship boutiques of designers like Cora Groppo (p113) and Nadine Zlotogora (p117). Upscale shopping centers like Alto Palermo (p107) also stock these designer lines, but you'll have to head to the boutiques along Recoleta's exclusive Av Alvear to find the true height of luxury. Discover more mainstream fashion along Av Santa Fe, the low-key streets of San Telmo, and the weekend designer fair circling Palermo's Plaza Serrano. Lusting after leather? Browse the shops in Retiro around Plaza San Martín and, if you have the patience for pushy salespeople, the leather stores along Microcentro's Florida and Lavalle streets. For a quieter scene and high-quality calf skin, head to Montserrat's leather outlets near the Mexico and San José intersection.

Check out the fashion section of the official **Buenos Aires tourism site** (www.bue.gov.ar) for more on recommended shopping venues and **Fashion Buenos Aires** (www.grupopampa.net/fba) for a comprehensive list of designers. Also look for excellent (and free) shopping maps of the city's various neighborhoods, available in businesses around town.

BEST FOR HER
> FFiocca (p73)
> Nadine Zlotogora (p117)
> Rapsodia (p118; pictured right)
> Josefina Ferroni (p97)
> Cora Groppo (p113)

BEST FOR HIM
> Felix (p116)
> Tramando (p97)
> Etiqueta Negra (p96)
> 28 Sport (p113)
> Hermanos Estebecorena (p116)

ESTANCIAS

Where have all the cowboys gone? You might find a gaucho getting rowdy in one of the city's *peñas*, but if you want to see some real silver spurs and leather chaps, you'll have to head for wide open spaces. The flat, rolling countryside surrounding the capital is dotted with ranches where you can encounter cowboy culture and gallop into the sunset astride an Argentine thoroughbred.

Dozens of *estancias*, or rural estates that were once the private geta-ways of wealthy porteño families, have opened their picket fences to the public. Many of these country hotels offer a *día de campo* (country day) that's ideal for day-trippers. One of the friendliest and most authentic options within easy reach of Buenos Aires is Estancia Los Dos Hermanos. You'll roll up to the farm for a country breakfast before mounting a horse and following the estancia's resident gaucho into the fields for a morning ride. Then it's back to the farmhouse for an alfresco *asado* (barbecue) and a quick hammock siesta before you hit the trails again for a few whiplash-inducing hours on horseback.

Rather hang your hat near the stables than race back to the city? *Estancia* accommodations range from luxurious suites with private fireplaces to rustic rooms with hardwood floors. Do your homework at www .estanciasargentinas.com – some *estancias* are just private homes that begrudgingly rent rooms for profit, others are campy circuses that bring in buses of camera-snapping tourists – but don't miss a chance to live out your cowboy dreams in the Argentine pampas.

BEST FOR A DAY TRIP
> Los Dos Hermanos (www.estancia losdoshermanos.com)
> La Figura (www.estancialafigura.com.ar)
> El Ombú de Areco (www.estancia elombu.com)

BEST FOR A COUNTRY WEEKEND
> Candelaria del Monte (www.candel ariadelmonte.com.ar)
> Mestiza Pampa Lodge (www.mestiza lodge.com)
> Juan Gerónimo (www.juangeronimo .com.ar)
> El Vinten (www.elvinten.com.ar)

ART

Porteño painters aren't exactly short on artistic inspiration. The clash of European and indigenous cultures, the aftermath of a brutal military government, the economic collapse of 2001 – local creative minds can take their pick from any number of hardships. Despite little support from the government, porteño artists are producing more provocative work than ever before.

Major museums like MALBA (p105) and the Museo Nacional de Bellas Artes (p86) are classic art venues, but most of the city's cutting-edge creations are on display in smaller galleries. Traditionally, the scene has been centered in Recoleta, with venues like Isabel Anchorena (see the boxed text, p94) attracting an old-school crowd of art patrons, though the circuit has expanded to include newer Palermo galleries as well, like Braga Menéndez (p60). The most important gallery, Fundación Proa (p86), is way off the beaten path in La Boca. Younger, edgier galleries can be found in San Telmo, like Zavaleta Lab (p60), and in Palermo Viejo. Excellent video and sculpture exhibits often occur, as well, at cultural centers like Centro Cultural Recoleta (p93).

What's Up Buenos Aires (www.whatsupbuenosaires.com) takes tourists into paint-splattered artists' workshops for a behind-the-scenes view. Also see www.arteamundo.com for exhibit reviews and pick up the *Mapa de las Artes* (Buenos Aires Arts Map), available at art museums, for the most comprehensive exhibition listings.

BEST ART MUSEUMS & CENTERS
> MALBA (p105)
> Museo Nacional de Bellas Artes (p94)
> Centro Cultural Borges (p39)
> Centro Cultural Recoleta (p93)
> Museo Nacional de Arte Decorativo (p106)

MOST HAPPENING GALLERIES BY BARRIO
> Fundación Proa (p86), La Boca
> Zavaleta Lab (p60), San Telmo
> Ruth Benzacar (p60), Microcentro
> Daniel Abate (p94), Recoleta
> Braga Menéndez Arte Contemporáneo (p60), Palermo Viejo

SPORTS

Monday night *fútbol*? Please – soccer is a household topic every day of the week in Buenos Aires. Virtually every man, woman and child in the city is fiercely loyal to one of two rival teams, River Plate or Boca Juniors, and the capital practically shuts down when they face off during the periodic Súperclasico match. Venture into the crowd of *barra brava* (soccer hooligans) with a tour operator like **Tangol** (www.tangol.com) that will make sure you're not sitting in the wrong section.

But there's more to local athletics than turf and penalty kicks. Argentina's national game, *pato* (duck; www.fedpato.com.ar), sees two teams of four men on horseback trying to throw a leather ball with handles (confused yet?) through a hoop at either end of a field. The nation's more famous for polo – and, admittedly, for the handsome polo players who star in Ralph Lauren print ads across the globe. Of course these upper-crust hunks have more to offer than chiseled cheekbones – their elegant horseback sport is on display at the Campo Argentino de Polo (p133) from September to mid-November. Similarly upper-class horseracing competitions are held at the historic Hipódromo Argentino (p133) – the spectators, gentlemen in tweed, couldn't be further removed the scrappy fans at La Bombonera (p89).

Boca Juniors or River Plate: which team will you choose at La Bombonera (p12)?

ARCHITECTURE

You don't have to know the difference between a cornice and a cantilever to see that Buenos Aires is an architectural wonderland. In this melting-pot South American capital, no one style prevails – thanks to a mix of influences from the Old World, art-nouveau apartment buildings rise up beside Italian Renaissance-style palaces.

The experimentation began when Argentina declared independence from Spain in 1816. Proud porteños rejected Spanish culture, which explains the city's relative dearth of colonial architecture except for a few examples like the Cabildo (p38) on Plaza de Mayo. Defiant architects adapted aesthetics from elsewhere in Europe – Italy, France and ancient Greece – to build the city's most magnificent structures. Teatro Colón (p60) was influenced by German, French and Italian Renaissance styles, while Mario Palanti borrowed both thematic and structural inspiration from his native Italy to build Palacio Barolo (p54). The famed Juan Buschiazzo added Doric columns to the entrance of the Cementerio de la Recoleta (p93) and an Italian facade to the Mercado de San Telmo (p75); meanwhile, many of the city's art-deco buildings display Latin American flair, like Otto Wulf's 1912 building on the corner of Perú and Belgrano in Montserrat, which features Indian figures and Argentine fauna.

The result of this haphazard design scheme is a thoroughly cosmopolitan, indigenous, nationalist architecture. The grandest stretch of jaw-dropping buildings, built between 1880 and 1930, runs along Av de Mayo. Start at Palacio del Congreso (p54) – don't miss the fabulous, decaying El Molino (p54) on the corner – and meander towards Plaza de Mayo.

MUST-SEE ANTIQUE STRUCTURES
> Palacio de las Aguas Corrientes (p54)
> Palacio Barolo (p54)
> Edificio Kavanagh (p64; pictured right)
> Mercado de Abasto (p108)

COOLEST CONTEMPORARY DESIGN
> Puente de la Mujer (p48)
> Floralis Genérica (p94)
> Faena Hotel + Universe (p51)
> Museo Xul Solar (p94)

BUENOS AIRES WITH KIDS

If the happy families and beautiful pregnant women crowding the streets of Buenos Aires are any indication, porteños adore children. Unlike in many cities, you won't be the object of disapproving glares if you deign to bring your little one into a 'nice' restaurant, and the city, though hectic and often filthy, abounds with children's activities and lovely parks where *los niños* (children) can let loose.

On weekends, Palermo fills with families. Popular activities include feeding the zany koi fish at the Jardín Japonés (p104), catching an astronomy show at the Planetario Galileo Galilei in the Parque 3 de Febrero (p107), and hitting up the petting zoo at the Jardín Zoológico (p104; pictured below). Shopping malls are like stroller-derbies on rainy days, and Abasto (p108) not only has great kids' shops, it also has the fantastic Museo de los Niños, filled with interactive activities to keep little hands occupied.

Whether or not a children's menu is offered, most cafes and restaurants welcome children and offer freshly squeezed juices, hot chocolate, and simple, kid-friendly foods like pizza and spaghetti. If you'd rather not subject fellow diners to the baby's crying, seek the company of other kid-toting families at eateries like the cafe at **Recursos Infantiles** (www.recursos infantiles.com.ar) or restaurants like **La Payuca** (www.lapayuca.com) that offer babysitter-staffed playrooms. Remember, porteños eat dinner late, but you can always pick up fresh fruit and *empanadas* between meal times.

Navigating Buenos Aires with kids, whether on foot or public transport, requires planning. Strollers are hard to steer through the busy sidewalks, buses are crowded, taxis are cramped – but rest assured, there's always a temper-taming ice-cream shop at your destination.

BEST KID-FRIENDLY SPOTS

> Jardín Zoológico (p104)
> Planetario Galileo Galilei at Parque 3 de Febrero (p107)
> Reserva Ecológica (p49)

A street vendor at La Boca's Caminito (p86)

BACKGROUND

HISTORY

Buenos Aires has had a tumultuous history, swinging between brutal dictatorships, prosperous periods, poverty and decades of military rule.

BUENOS AIRES TODAY

Buenos Aires lives with the scars of several economic crashes, most notably the collapse in 2001. It's hard to overstate how badly these struggles have affected the porteño (BA local) psyche. Hardworking professionals lost their savings, families had to give up their houses and move into smaller apartments, and national pride was damaged as Argentina's international status tumbled. Things started to look up for Buenos Aires residents after the election of ex-president Nestor Kirchner, who restructured Argentina's debt and brought sustainable growth to the country during his 2003–2007 term. Kirchner endeavored to reconcile the country with its past, revoking the immunity of military officials who participated in the 'Dirty War' and facilitating trials of war criminals.

Kirchner's wife, former senator Cristina Fernández de Kirchner, succeeded her husband when she was elected as Argentina's president in October 2007. Though she's continued the economic programs her husband started, she's a controversial figure who's spent much of her professional energy battling the province's farmers over taxation issues and trying to maintain social stability in the face of inflation and skyrocketing job losses, partly caused by the international economic crisis that began in 2008.

Meanwhile, the Madres of Plaza de Mayo (see also p17) continue their campaign to identify the children of the *desaparecidos* (disappeared ones). During the Dirty War, the military captured (and later murdered) thousands of young parents, whose babies were then distributed among military families. Many of these children (they're adults now, in their thirties) are unaware of their own lineage and the fact that their 'parents' are, in fact, ex-military families deeply involved in one of the country's bloodiest eras. Newspaper notices urge young people who feel any suspicions about their own parentage to come forward and begin the terrifying process of investigating his or her own family history. Though a handful of these children of the *desaparecidos* have uncovered the truth and been reunited with their actual relatives, many are understandably reluctant to acknowledge any such suspicions, and the subject remains a tense one.

BACKWATER PORT TURNS CAPITAL

Buenos Aires was founded twice. Spaniard Pedro de Mendoza's 1536 settlement failed after settlers were ousted by the indigenous Querandí, who had populated the Río de la Plata banks for tens of thousands of years. Juan de Garay re-established Buenos Aires in 1580, though it remains unclear exactly where in the city he planted the Spanish flag.

The town remained a backwater as the Spanish Crown focused its empire-building on silver-rich Alto Perú, restricting trade through Buenos Aires. As a result, local merchants turned to contraband. By 1776, the increasing wealth passing through the port finally forced Spain to make BA the capital of the new Viceroyalty of the Río de la Plata.

INDEPENDENCE & THE GOLDEN AGE

The British attempted to claim Buenos Aires in 1806 and 1807, but the locals beat them back to their ships, pouring cauldrons of boiling oil and water from rooftops and firing cannons from balconies. The successful expulsion gave *criollos* (Argentine-born colonists) new confidence to stand up to Spain, and they declared independence on May 25, 1810. Formal independence for Argentina was declared in Tucumán on July 9, 1816.

After a lengthy civil war, a succession of presidents and the creation of Argentina's constitution, the country moved into a golden age of prosperity that lasted from the late 1800s until 1929. During this time, many fine buildings were built. Between 1869 and 1895, European immigrants flooded in, increasing the city's population sevenfold. Industry was unable to absorb this mass immigration and labor unrest grew. With the onset of the Great Depression, the military took power under conditions of considerable social unease. An obscure colonel, Juan Domingo Perón, was the first leader to face Argentina's economic crisis.

PERÓN TO ALFONSÍN

Juan Perón, with help from his charismatic wife, Eva (Evita) Perón (p93), became president in 1946. While the power couple had their critics, the Peróns also championed working-class causes and introduced social justice and welfare. Criticism regarding Perón's dictatorial demeanor, economic difficulties and Evita's 1952 death undermined Perón's second presidency, and in late 1955 a military coup exiled him to Spain, initiating nearly three decades of catastrophic military rule.

Perón returned to Argentina in 1973, became president again, and died a year later. On March 24, 1976, a military coup took control of the government, bringing General Jorge Videla to power and beginning the period known as the 'Dirty War.' In late 1980 Videla stepped down in favor of army general Roberto Viola, who served a year. He was followed by army commander-in-chief General Leopoldo Galtieri.

By 1982, the military dictatorship began to lose legitimacy, and in an attempt to drum up support, the government launched an invasion to dislodge the British from the Falkland Islands, which Argentina claimed as its own. Underestimating a strong British response, Argentina surrendered after 74 days. The military regime was left in tatters and civilian Raúl Alfonsín was elected president in 1983. Human-rights groups estimate that some 30,000 people were killed or 'disappeared' between 1976 and 1983.

THE DOWNWARD SPIRAL

Carlos Ménem succeeded Alfonsín in 1989, inheriting hyperinflation and a recession. He solved this by ushering in a 'golden age' of false economic stability, largely thanks to pegging the peso to the US dollar. Fiscal irresponsibility and rampant government corruption left state coffers nearly empty by 1999. By 2001 the economy teetered on collapse. Amid nationwide protests (the biggest occurred in BA) over a government freeze on bank withdrawals, Ménem's successor, Fernando de la Rúa (formerly BA's mayor), resigned. Three interim presidents had also resigned by the time Eduardo Duhalde was chosen as caretaker president in January 2002. Duhalde devalued the peso and announced that Argentina would default on its US$140 billion foreign debt. Nestor Kirchner won office in the May 2003 elections.

GOVERNMENT & POLITICS

Officially known as the Ciudad Autónoma de Buenos Aires, BA is the capital of Argentina. The title denotes its standing as an independent district (similar to Washington, DC). The provincial capital is La Plata, 60km east.

Traditionally Argentina's president appointed the mayor of Buenos Aires, but constitutional reform in 1996 permitted Fernando de la Rúa to become the city's first elected mayor. The following two-term mayor, Aníbal Ibarra, was impeached and removed from office in 2006 for negligence after an inquiry into a nightclub blaze that killed almost 200 people in 2004. The current mayor, Mauricio Macri, was well-known before his election as mayor as the president of the Boca Juniors *fútbol* club. A capitalist and the son of an international entrepreneur, he has announced his future interest in running for the presidency of Argentina.

Politics in Buenos Aires is also played out on the streets, most visibly manifesting itself in the almost-daily protests around Plaza de Mayo (p40). Generally peaceful, these protests are carried out by groups of *piqueteros* (picketers) who block city streets, making demands or commemorating political events.

ECONOMY

When 'convertibility' (pegging the peso to the US dollar) was scrapped and the government announced it would convert bank accounts at a rate of 1.4 pesos per dollar, everyone with money still in Argentine banks lost over half their dollar value. For most Argentines, this was a disaster. Argentina's sizable middle class was ruined, and today almost half of BA's population lives below the poverty line. Although the employment rates have gone up a bit in the last few years, inflation has complicated the financial affairs of many porteños.

Former president Nestor Kirchner finished restructuring Argentina's debt, and at the end of his term, the economy was looking strong. Growth slowed during the start of Cristina Fernández de Kirchner's presidency – and matters weren't helped any by the worldwide economic crisis that started at the end of 2008. The socioeconomic problems caused by the huge divide between rich and poor remain unresolved, a fact that's on obvious display every evening at sunset. Just before the garbage trucks roll through the city, bands of *cartoneros* (poor porteños who scour garbage looking for cardboard, glass and other recyclables they can exchange for money) rifle through the trash bags waiting on the street. The sight of small immigrant children poking through coffee grounds and discarded newspapers assures you, if there was any doubt, that Argentina's economy has a long way to go.

ENVIRONMENT

Considering that Argentina is home to pristine wine regions, the glaciers of Patagonia and pastures of grass-fed cows stretching as far as the eye can see, tourists might expect Buenos Aires to be more eco-friendly than it actually is. Despite its position at the mouth of the Río de la Plata, on the eastern edge of the vast Argentine grasslands known as the Pampas, Buenos Aires is a megacity suffering from various types of pollution and environmental problems resulting from overpopulation. Noise (honking cars and roaring buses) and air pollution are factors of everyday life.

TUMMY-TUCKS & TANGO
If you have a friend who comes back from Buenos Aires looking refreshed, relaxed and – how to put this? – better endowed, she might not have simply been taking tango lessons. When Argentina's economic woes began, plastic surgery was already wildly popular with locals, and with surgery available at around a third of US and European costs, 'health tourism' is very popular. A trip usually consists of a few nights in Buenos Aires, followed by a procedure ranging from gluteoplasty to the ever-popular breast implants. You didn't think that *all* of the women here were naturally beautiful, did you?

Fortunately, frequent rains clear the smoggy air. City streets are often smattered with dog poop, especially in the city's south, making for an occasionally slippery and smelly walk.

Buenos Aires' waterways – most visibly the Riachuelo in the barrio of La Boca – are contaminated by local industry. Despite Argentina's self-sufficiency in petroleum and hydroelectricity, the government has promoted nuclear power since 1950. The city lacks an official recycling system, though a huge number of *cartoneros* make their living picking through city trash for anything they can sell to recycling centers.

LIFE AS A PORTEÑO

Buenos Aires is one of Latin America's most cosmopolitan cities. Between 1870 and 1920, over six million people immigrated to Argentina, the majority settling in BA. Most came from Spain and Italy, and also from Britain, Portugal, France and Eastern Europe post-WWII, bringing with them food, football and music. Middle Eastern and Asian immigrants also arrived.

Catholicism remains the official religion and while most porteños don't attend mass, they dangle rosaries from their rearview mirrors and cross themselves when passing churches.

Porteños are remarkably friendly. Stopping someone to ask directions is normal and often leads to friendly conversation about your origin and why you're in Buenos Aires. Many porteños speak some English and love the chance to practice. Although BA is known for its fashionable residents, the look is surprisingly casual – the key is to look clean and neat, not like you just rolled out of bed and down to the corner coffee shop.

During introductions, women exchange cheek kisses (one on each) and men shake hands. Among friends, men kiss cheeks too. Always exchange pleasantries – a *buenos días* (good morning) or *buenas tardes* (good afternoon) at minimum – with people you meet in elevators and shops and with taxi drivers.

ARTS

ARCHITECTURE

Buenos Aires boasts a fascinating mix of architecture and is one of the world's best cities for design students and lovers of all things architectural. See p149 for more.

LITERATURE

Argentina's capital has long been a literary city, with bookstores, newsstands, book fairs and authors aplenty and a wealth of elegant cafes where you can get lost in a good novel. The most fitting place to start your reading is Jorge Luis Borges (1899–1986), one of the 20th century's greatest writers. He penned fiction, nonfiction and poetry, much of which is set just outside his former home in Buenos Aires. His stories are amassed into the tome *Collected Fictions,* which is translated into English – look for the Norman Thomas di Giovanni translation, which is superior to the later one.

Another 20th-century great is the bohemian Julio Cortázar (1914–84), a porteño writer who defected to Paris – but not before his *Rayuela* (Hopscotch) was deemed a milestone in modern fiction. Cortázar's inventive, nonlinear narrative invites readers to choose between two paths. Also of the Borges generation is Ernesto Sábato (1911–), whose complex and uncompromising novels have profoundly influenced Argentine literature. Other notable porteño writers include Adolfo Bioy Casares and sisters Silvina and Victoria Ocampo.

José Hernández (1834–1886) wasn't a porteño, but he did write one of the country's most important books, *Martín Fierro* (1872), an epic poem about gaucho life. It's sold in a variety of languages.

FURTHER READING

> *Asleep in the Sun* (2004; Adolfo Bioy Casares)
> *The Buenos Aires Affair* (1973; Manuel Puig)
> *Heartbreak Tango* (1969; Manuel Puig)
> *The Invention of Morel* (2003; Adolfo Bioy Casares)
> *Labyrinths: Selected Stories & Other Writings* (2007; Jorge Luis Borges)
> *On Heroes and Tombs* (1981; Ernesto Sabato)

FILM

Argentina has a long cinematic tradition (producing its first film in 1897) and a history of cinematically sophisticated movies. In the 1930s and '40s, popular genres included *tangueras* (tango-centered musicals) and gaucho Western films. You'll see these available for purchase at street kiosks.

Films of the 1960s and '70s were politically radical, such as Fernando Solanas and Octavio Getino's powerful, four-hour leftist documentary *La Hora de los Hornos* (The Hour of the Furnaces; 1968). A more mellow Solanas won Best Director at Cannes in 1988 for his mesmerizing *Sur* (South), and acclaim for his documentary *La Dignidad de los Nadies* (Dignity of the Nobodies; 2005) about the impact of the economic crisis on everyday life. For an insight into the Dirty War, see Luis Puenzo's *The Official Story* (1985), which won a Best Foreign-language Film Oscar.

Recent decades have seen a uniquely Latin American magic realism appear in films such as Eliseo Subiela's *Hombre Mirando al Sureste* (Man Facing Southeast; 1985), and melodramas by feminists such as María Luisa Bemberg and Lucrecia Martel. Martel's films *La Cienaga* (The Swamp; 2001) and *La Niña Santa* (The Holy Girl; 2004) offer insights into the complexities of Argentine relationships.

MUSIC

Tango (see also p138) is the heart and soul of porteño music, but there are many styles of music worth exploring in BA. Argentina's folk music is called *folklórica*. Styles such as *chamamé, chacarera,* samba and the *carnavlito* are all beautiful mixes of traditional Andean music and old European rhythms. BA's many *peñas* (folk venues) are the places to hear

---

MOVIE MEMENTOS

These award-winning contemporary films capture quotidian life in Buenos Aires. Some are available internationally, others you'll find in the city's music and book stores (all have subtitles):

> *Nueve Reinas* (Nine Queens; 2000) – Fabián Bielinsky
> *El Hijo de la Novia* (Son of the Bride; 2001) – Juan José Campanella
> *El Bonaerense* (2002) – Pablo Trapero
> *Historias Mínimas* (Minimal Stories; 2002) – Carlos Solin
> *Assassination Tango* (2002) – Robert Duvall
> *Crónica de una Fuga* (Chronicle of an Escape; 2006) – Adrian Caetano
> *Derecho de Familia* (Family Law; 2007) – Daniel Burman
> *Quién Dice Que es Fácil¿* (Who Says it's Easy?; 2007) -- Juan Taratuto

this infectious music. Arguably the nation's greatest *folklórica* singer was Atahulapa Yupanqui, who influenced later *nueva canción* (new song movement) musicians including the astounding Mercedes Sosa and Los Chalchaleros.

Argentina has also had a rich rock-and-roll heritage (called *rock nacional*; national rock) dating back to the 1960s – check out the Beatles-esque Los Shakers. Musicians such as Fito Páez and Charlie García (one half of influential '70s folk-rock group Sui Generis) are national icons. In the 1980s, the hugely influential Soda Stereo was Argentina's version of The-Police-meets-Duran-Duran. Contemporary performers include Bersuit Vergarabat and Kevin Johansen (born in Alaska to an Argentine mother). Johansen's music is like Leonard Cohen fused with Argentine folk.

VISUAL ART

Xul Solar (1887–1963) was one of Argentina's most visionary modern artists, his work aligned with fauvist, expressionist, constructivist and cubist movements. Another renowned painter was Antonio Berni (1905–81), a neofigurative and impressionist artist who painted everyday scenes exploring socioeconomic inequality. The Galerías Pacífico (p40) ceiling features his murals. Benito Quinquela Martín (1890–1977) was a popular artist who put the working-class barrio of La Boca on the artistic map, painting vivid scenes of port life. The former homes of both Quinquela and Solar are now museums displaying their work (see p86 and p94).

Argentina's 2001 economic crisis triggered a tidal wave of ideas and output from BA's contemporary artists, and while there's little public support, many are making a living through commercial galleries and foreign sales. There are scores of small galleries in San Telmo, Recoleta, Retiro and Palermo. For comprehensive gallery listings, pick up a copy of *Mapa de Las Artes* (BA Art Map) from MALBA (p105) or most other art museums.

DIRECTORY
TRANSPORTATION

Hoof it, hop on the bus, take a taxi or descend into the Subte (subway) system – there's no shortage of transportation options in Buenos Aires. While some options are more glamorous than others, all are reliable and cheap by international standards.

ARRIVAL & DEPARTURE
AIR
Aeropuerto Internacional Ministro Pistarini (EZE; ☎ 5480-6111; www.aa2000.com.ar),

better known as Ezeiza, is where nearly all international flights arrive. Left luggage is available next to the Farmacity store on the ground floor of Level A.

Domestic flights and flights to/from Uruguay leave from **Aeroparque Jorge Newbery** (AEP; ☎ 5480-6111; www.aa2000.com.ar; Av Costanera Rafael Obligado, Costanera Norte), a short distance from downtown.

Ezeiza
Traveling the 35km from the airport to town takes about 45 minutes by cab or shuttle, and up to 1½ hours by bus.

Transport Times Between Neighborhoods

	Microcentro	Puerto Madero	Congreso & Tribunales
Microcentro	n/a	walk 10min	walk 10min, Subte 5min
Puerto Madero	walk 10min	n/a	taxi 10-15min, Subte 5min
Congreso & Tribunales	walk 10min, Subte 5min	taxi 10-15 min, Subte 5min	n/a
Retiro	walk 5min	walk 10-15min	walk 10min, Subte 5min
San Telmo	walk 15min	walk 10-15min	walk 15-20min, taxi 5min
La Boca	taxi 15min, bus 25min	taxi 10min	taxi 15min
Recoleta & Barrio Norte	walk 15-20min, taxi 5-10min	taxi 15min	taxi 10min
Palermo	taxi 20min, Subte 15min	taxi 25min, Subte 20min	taxi 15-20min Subte 10-15min

Public bus 86 ($1.35) makes the slow slog into town – only take it if you're really pinching pennies. You can catch the bus outside the Aerolíneas Argentinas terminal, a short walk from the international terminal. **Manuel Tienda León** (MTL; ☎ 0810-888-5366; www.tiendaleon.com) offers fast, fairly priced shuttle buses to/from downtown ($40) every 30 minutes. Hotel drop-off/pickup is free within the city center; if your hotel is elsewhere, take the service to/from the **downtown office** (Map p63, D2; ☎ 4314-3636; Av Madero 1299 at San Martín, Retiro). MTL's airport office sits directly outside customs.

Avoid the freestanding vehicles and people shouting 'taxi!' around the airport. Always take an official taxi or *remise* – these can be booked at stands in the arrival hall and will cost you about $100.

Aeroparque Jorge Newbery

Public buses 33 and 45 ($0.80) run to the center (don't cross the street when you exit the airport, take them going south). MTL shuttles also run to the center ($15). A taxi to the center costs about $20.

BUS

Buenos Aires' **Retiro Bus Terminal** (Map p63, D1; ☎ 4310-0700; www.tebasa.com.ar,

Retiro	San Telmo	La Boca	Recoleta & Barrio Norte	Palermo
walk 5min	walk 15min	taxi 15min, bus 25min	walk 15-20min, taxi 5-10min	taxi 20min, Subte 15min
walk 10-15min	walk 10-15min	taxi 10min	taxi 15min	taxi 25min, Subte 20min
walk 10min, Subte 5min	walk 15-20min, taxi 5min	taxi 15min	taxi 10min	taxi 15-20min, Subte 10-15min
n/a	walk 25min, taxi 10min	taxi 20min	taxi 10min	taxi 10-15min, Subte 15min
walk 25min, taxi 10min	n/a	taxi 10min	taxi 15min	taxi 20-25min
taxi 20min	taxi 10min	n/a	taxi 20min	taxi 25min
taxi 10min	taxi 15min	taxi 20min	n/a	walk 10-30min, taxi 5-15min
taxi 10-15min, Subte 15min	taxi 20-25min	taxi 25min	walk 10-30min, taxi 5-15min	n/a

in Spanish; Av Ramos Mejía 1680, Retiro) offers bus connections to/from cities in Argentina and most South American capitals. Hundreds of bus companies serve Retiro (not to be confused with nearby Estación Retiro train station) – head to the information desk or check the website for destination info. Long-distance buses range from comfortable to luxurious (*cama suite* class includes champagne and nearly fully reclining seats for overnight trips). Make sure you get a luggage claim ticket and be sure to tip the handler.

Retiro is walking distance from the north end of calle Florida; a cab from here to anywhere in the center costs around $15.

BOAT

There are several river crossings between Uruguay and Buenos Aires via ferry or hydrofoil; some trips also involve buses. Ferries leave from the following locations:

Buquebus Terminal (Map p47, A2; ☎ 4316-6500; www.buquebus.com; Av Antártida Argentina & Córdoba, Puerto Madero).

Colonia del Sacramento Daily ferries (one-way from $93, three hours) and hydrofoils (one-way from $130, one hour), with direct bus connections to Montevideo (three hours more).

Montevideo Daily high-speed ferries from BA to Montevideo (one-way from $241, three hours).

Punta del Este Daily hydrofoils from BA to Colonia connecting with direct bus service to Punta del Este (one-way from $192, five hours) and daily high-speed ferries from BA to Montevideo connecting with direct bus service to Punta del Este (one-way from $283, five hours).

TRAVEL DOCUMENTS

Passports must be valid for six months from date of entry.

VISA

Nationals of Australia, USA, Canada, New Zealand and most Western European countries do not need visas to visit Argentina, and you are allowed to stay for 90 days. At the start of 2009, Argentina, like some other South American countries, instated

CLIMATE CHANGE & TRAVEL

Travel – especially air travel – is a significant contributor to global climate change. At Lonely Planet, we believe that all who travel have a responsibility to limit their personal impact. As a result, we have teamed with Rough Guides and other concerned industry partners to support Climate Care, which allows people to offset the greenhouse gases they are responsible for with contributions to energy-saving projects and other climate-friendly initiatives in the developing world. Lonely Planet offsets all staff and author travel.

For more information, turn to the responsible travel pages on www.lonelyplanet .com. For details on offsetting your carbon emissions and a carbon calculator, go to www .climatecare.org.

a 'reciprocity fee' that charges incoming US tourists an amount similar to what Argentine citizens pay for an American visa (currently about US$135).

RETURN/ONWARD TICKET

A return/onward ticket is officially required but rarely requested.

DEPARTURE TAX

An international departure tax is levied on flights leaving Argentina. After checking in to your flight in the departures hall at Ezeiza, you'll have to pay the tax in US dollars (US$22), Argentine pesos or euros and have the tax sticker placed on your ticket.

GETTING AROUND

With an underground subway (the Subte), a 24-hour bus system and a plethora of affordable taxis, Buenos Aires is easy to get around. The capital is a very walkable city, but when you need to cover a sizeable distance, the Subte or a cab is your best bet. Relying on public transport requires a bit of initial study. In this book, the nearest Subte or bus line is noted after the Ⓜ or 🚍 icon for each listing.

BUS

The city has a huge and complex *colectivo* (bus) system, but it's not particularly user-friendly for foreigners – stops aren't announced,

you need several coins to ride, and if you don't have a good idea where you're getting off, the bus will fly right past your destination. The only way to make any sense of the system is to purchase a *Guia T* (bus guidebook), available at kiosks throughout the city. Locate your destination street in the index, flip to the indicated map page and grid box, then match a bus number from that box to your departure box. Most rides cost around $1.25. Get on the bus with a handful of change and tell the driver the name of your stop, insert the coins into the machine and wait for a ticket to pop out. Coins are scarce in BA, making bus travel tricky – there's talk of starting a more contemporary card system that doesn't involve small change, but no progress had been made at the time of research.

SUBTE

BA's **Subte** (☎ 0800-555-1616; www .subte.com.ar, in Spanish) opened in 1913 and is the quickest way to get around the city. In summer – and at rush hour – the cars are hot and crowded, so be sure to watch your valuables. Single-ride magnetic cards cost $1.10 and can be purchased at *boleterías* (ticket booths) in all Subte stations. To save time, buy a five- or 10-ride card, since queues can get backed up. At some stations, the tracks separate the platforms, so make sure of your direction before passing through the turnstiles. Trains operate between 5am and 10:30pm from Monday to Saturday; and from 8am to 10pm on Sunday. Service is frequent on weekdays, slower on weekends.

TRAIN

For getting around the city, the only train that really comes in handy is the Mitre line, which makes getting from Retiro to Las Cañitas or Belgrano's Chinatown a snap. At the ticket window inside Estación Retiro (Map p63, C2) ask for tickets ($2) to Belgrano station on the Mitre line.

TAXI & REMISE

BA's black-and-yellow taxis ply the city day and night; you rarely have to wait long to hail one. To avoid any trouble with counterfeit notes or dodgy drivers, hail a taxi with the words 'radio taxi,' indicating that the vehicle is part of a licensed agency. The starting fare is $3.80, and drivers should always use the *taxímetro* (taxi meter). Tipping is not expected, but leave the small change. Most rides within one area of the city cost around $12, up to around $20 across the city. Call **Pidalo** (☎ 4956-1200) or **Radio Taxi Premium** (☎ 4374-6666).

Remises (radio taxis) look like regular cars and don't have meters. They cost about the same

as street taxis, but you're less likely to get ripped off because the fare is always established beforehand. Most hotels and restaurants will call a *remise* for you; it's also a handy way to get to the airport. Try **Remises Blue** (☎ 4777-8888).

PRACTICALITIES
BUSINESS HOURS

General business hours for offices are from 8am to 5pm, Monday to Friday. Shopping centers generally operate from 10am to 10pm daily. Most stores stay open until 7pm or 9pm on weekdays, and open from 9am to 1pm or 2pm on Saturdays. Popular shopping areas such as Palermo open on Sundays as well. Most banks close by 4pm on weekdays, and are open on Saturdays from 9am to 1pm. Restaurants generally open daily from noon to 3:30pm for lunch, and from 8pm to midnight or later for dinner. Cafes are open from early morning until after 8pm, often much later. Tourist offices open from 8am or 9am to between 8pm and 10pm daily.

DISCOUNTS
STUDENT & YOUTH CARDS

The International Student Identity Card (ISIC) – available for US$13 through the student and discount travel agency **Asatej** (Map p37, B2; ☎ 4114-7500; www.asatej.net, in Spanish;

Room 320, 3rd fl, Galería Buenos Aires, Florida 835, Microcentro; 🕙 9am-7pm Mon-Fri) – can help travelers obtain discounts on museum admissions.

SENIORS' DISCOUNTS

Travelers over the age of 60 can sometimes obtain senior-citizen discounts on museum admissions and the like. Usually a passport with date of birth is sufficient evidence of age. There are no seniors' cards in Argentina.

ELECTRICITY

Argentina operates on 220V AC 50Hz. There are two types of electric plugs: those with two round prongs (as in Europe) and those with three angled, flat prongs (as in Australia and New Zealand). To use a US laptop that doesn't have a built-in 110V to 220V converter you'll need a transformer and an adaptor. The transformer must be rated for electronic equipment – converters sold at most travel stores are for hairdryers or battery chargers and can fry your machine! Both are available at *ferreterías* (hardware stores) throughout the city.

EMERGENCIES

As in any big city, there are rough neighborhoods in BA, and while most of the areas with tourist appeal are generally fine, they also attract pickpockets. After all,

if George W Bush's daughter can have her handbag stolen in San Telmo while being protected by bodyguards, so can you! Be careful in markets and while watching tango on the streets – pickpockets love it when you're preoccupied. Walking around with a digital SLR camera screams 'rich tourist,' which makes you a more attractive target for pickpockets. While San Telmo is safe during the day, be cautious at night, and always be cautious in La Boca – take a taxi. When it comes to scams, you'll get the occasional taxi driver who'll take you for a longer ride than necessary, and there are counterfeit bank notes floating around. Don't give a taxi driver $100 unless you want to check every piece of change.

In case of an emergency:

Ambulance (☎ 107)
Fire (☎ 100)
Police (☎ 101)
Rape crisis line (☎ 4981-6882, 4958-4291)
Tourist police (☎ 4346-5748, 0800-999-5000)

HOLIDAYS

Año Nuevo (New Year's Day) January 1
Holy Thursday and Good Friday/Easter March/April
Día de Trabajador (Labor Day) May 1
Revolución de Mayo (May Revolution) May 25
Día de las Malvinas (Malvinas Day) June 10
Día de la Bandera (Flag Day) June 20
Día de la Independencia (Independence Day) July 9

Día de San Martín (date of San Martín's death) August 17
Día de la Raza (Columbus Day) October 12
Día de la Tradición (Day of Tradition) November 10
Día de la Concepción Inmaculada (Immaculate Conception Day) December 8
Navidad (Christmas Day) December 25

....

INTERNET

Throughout this book most of the websites listed are in Spanish only, but even if your Spanish is basic, most sites are easy to glean information from. Lonelyplanet .com offers speedy links to many BA websites. Other useful sites:
Buenos Aires Herald (www.buenosaires herald.com) Online portal of BA's English-language daily.
Clarín (www.clarin.com.ar, in Spanish) Argentina's largest-circulation daily.
La Nación (www.lanacion.com.ar, in Spanish) BA's oldest and most prestigious daily.
Óleo (www.guiaoleo.com.ar, in Spanish) Extensive online guide to BA restaurants.
Secretaría de Turismo (www.turismo .gob.ar) The national tourist board's official Argentina website.
Subsecretaría de Turismo (www.bue.gov .ar) BA's official tourism website.
What's Up Buenos Aires (www.whatsup buenosaires.com) Tune in to what's going down in BA.

....

LANGUAGE

Argentine Spanish, referred to locally as *castellano* (*rioplatense*), is heavily influenced by Italian, especially in BA. Unlike other Latin Americans, Argentines use the second-person *voseo* form (*vos* instead of *tú*). Porteño (BA local) Spanish is further complicated by Lunfardo, the slang rooted in Italian and often found in tango lyrics. Lunfardo words you'll hear include *che* (dude), *piola* (cool), *pucho* (cigarette), *morfar* (to eat) and *bondi* (bus). *Boludo* (jerk, idiot) is a favorite insult, often used in a friendly fashion. Lonely Planet's *Latin American Spanish* phrasebook is handy to have along.

BASICS

Hello.	*Hola.*
Goodbye.	*Adiós./Chau.*
Please.	*Por favor.*
Thank you.	*Gracias.*
How are you?	*¿Qué tal?*
I'm fine (thanks).	*Bien, gracias.*
Excuse me.	*Perdón.*
Yes.	*Sí.*
No.	*No.*
Thank you (very much).	*(Muchas) gracias.*
You're welcome.	*De nada./Con mucho gusto.*
Do you speak English?	*¿Habla inglés?*
I don't understand.	*No entiendo.*
How much is it?	*¿Cuánto vale?*
That's too expensive.	*Es demasiado caro.*

EATING & DRINKING

That was delicious!	*¡Estaba buenísimo!*

I'm a vegetarian.	*Soy vegetariano/a. (m/f)*
Please bring the bill.	*La cuenta, por favor.*

EMERGENCIES

I'm sick.	*Estoy enfermo/a. (m/f)*
Help!	*¡Socorro!*
Call the police!	*¡Llame a la policía!*
Call an ambulance!	*¡Llame a una ambulancia!*

DAYS & NUMBERS

today	*hoy*
tonight	*esta noche*
tomorrow	*mañana*
0	*cero*
1	*unos*
2	*dos*
3	*tres*
4	*cautro*
5	*cinco*
6	*seis*
7	*siete*
8	*ocho*
9	*nueve*
10	*diez*
11	*once*
12	*doce*
21	*veintiuno*
100	*cien*
1000	*mil*

MONEY

Argentina's currency is the peso (simply denoted as $ in this book).

Bills come in denominations of two, five, 10, 20, 50 and 100 pesos. One peso equals 100 centavos; coins come in denominations of five, 10, 25 and 50 centavos, and one peso. Changing a $50 or $100 bill at kiosks or smaller businesses is nearly always impossible, so change it whenever the chance arises, and watch out for counterfeit large notes.

Leave traveler's checks at home – hardly anyone accepts them. Some restaurants (even some well-known ones) don't accept credit cards, so always check first. When using credit cards at supermarkets and shopping centers, cashiers may ask for photo identification. ATMs are everywhere in BA, but they can run out of money quickly on weekends.

NEWSPAPERS & MAGAZINES

The capital's biggest daily newspapers are *Clarín* and *La Nación*; the only English-language daily is the *Buenos Aires Herald*. For sports news, pick up *Olé*. For opinionated leftist news, pick up *Página 12*. If you're craving English magazines, apart from *Time* and *Newsweek* at some newsstands, you're pretty much out of luck.

ORGANIZED TOURS

Fascinating architecture, neighborhood, soccer, history, art and cultural tours are available. The following tour companies have English-speaking guides – just let them know that you need one.

BA Local (☎ 4554-1877; www.balocal.com) Stylish, tailor-made excursions into BA's fashion, dining and cultural scenes with an ex-New Yorker (see also boxed text, p116).

Cicerones (☎ 4330-0800; www.cicerones.org.ar) A nonprofit (and free) organization that matches visitors' language needs and interests with one of its porteño volunteers.

Eternautas (☎ 4384-7874; www.eternautas.com) Thematic urban tours such as 'Evita' and 'Perónism,' plus full-day tours and excursions.

Jewish Tours Argentina (www.jewish-tours.com.ar) Personalized tours through the city's Jewish past with a knowledgeable local guide.

La Bicicleta Naranja (☎ 4362-1104; www.labicicletanaranja.com.ar) Bike rentals and a good range of organized bike tours.

Tangol (☎ 4312-7276; www.tangol.com) Long-standing operator offering the best fútbol (soccer) tours.

Urban Biking (☎ 4568-4321; www.urbanbiking.com) One-day cycling tours – including an alternative 'nightlife' bike trip – and bike & kayak excursions to Tigre.

TELEPHONE

Two companies, Telecom and Telefónica, split the city's telephone services. The easiest way to make a local call is to find a *locutorio* (small telephone office), where you call from a private cabin and pay at the register when you're through. There's a *locutorio* on practically every other block – they cost about the same as street phones, are much quieter and you won't run out of coins. Most *locutorios* are supplied with phone books. The main cell phone systems are CDMA and TDMA. It's now possible to use a tri-band GSM world cell phone in BA, and you can buy SIM cards to use locally. If you're just here for a few days you can rent a cell phone – Tangol (see p168) will even deliver it and pick it up again before you leave the city.

COUNTRY & CITY CODES

All telephone numbers in the greater Buenos Aires area have eight digits; cell phone numbers are always preceded by an extra '15.' Argentina's country code is ☎ 54, and the area code for BA is ☎ 011. If calling from abroad, dial your country's code before 54 11 and the eight digits, or, if you're calling a cell phone, 54 911 and the last eight digits.

Toll-free numbers begin with ☎ 0800 or ☎ 0810.

USEFUL PHONE NUMBERS

Directory assistance (☎ 110)
International direct-dial code (☎ 00 + country code)
International operator (☎ 000)
Telecom/Telefónica service (☎ 112)

TIPPING

Unless the service is truly horrible, tip 10% on restaurant tabs, even when a *cubierto* (silverware and bread charge) is included. Bartenders are occasionally tipped, and they often ring a bar bell when it happens. Leave cab drivers the small change.

TOURIST INFORMATION

The **Secretaría de Turismo de la Nación** (Map p63, B3; ☎ 4312-2232; www .turismo.gob.ar; Av Santa Fe 883, Microcentro; ☼ 9am-5pm Mon-Fri) provides information on BA and Argentina. The **Comisaría del Turista** (Map p37, C3; Tourist Police; ☎ 4346-5748, 0800-999-5000; turista@policia.federal.gov.ar; Av Corrientes 436, Microcentro; ☼ 24hr) provides interpreters and helps crime victims.

Several of the city's tourist kiosks do not have telephones (or sometimes anyone who speaks English!), but there is a toll-free **tourist information line** (☎ 0800-555-0016; ☼ 8am-8pm). Tourist kiosk locations:

Aeroparque airport (☎ 4773-9805; ☼ 8am-8pm)

Ezeiza airport (☎ 4480-0224; ☼ 8am-8pm)

Microcentro (Map p37, B4; cnr Florida & Diagonal Roque Sáenz Peña; Microcentro; ☼ 9am-6pm Mon-Sat)

Puerto Madero (Map p47, A2; ☎ 4313-0187; Dique 4, Puerto Madero; ☼ 11am-6pm Mon-Fri, to 7pm Sat)

Recoleta (Map p91, E2; Av Quintana 596, Recoleta; ☼ 10:30am-6:30pm Mon-Fri, 10am-7pm Sat & Sun)

Retiro (Map p63, C3; Florida & Marcelo T de Alvear, Retiro; ☼ 10am-7pm)

Retiro Bus Terminal (Map p63, D1; ☎ 4311-0528; Ste 83, 2nd fl, Av Ramos Mejía 1680, Retiro; ☼ 7:30am-1pm Mon-Sat)

TRAVELERS WITH DISABILITIES

Travelers with disabilities will find getting around BA difficult but not impossible. Negotiating the city's narrow, busy and uneven sidewalks in a wheelchair can be a challenge. Crossing streets can be tricky, since not every corner has ramps, and Argentine drivers have little patience. Nevertheless, Argentines with disabilities do get around, and there are a few *piso bajo* (lowered floor for wheelchair lifts) buses.

Throughout this book, listings marked with a ⅋ icon are wheelchair accessible. Every place is different, of course, but as a general guideline we have included the icon where access is relatively easy.

INFORMATION & ORGANIZATIONS

In Buenos Aires, **Movidisc** (Map p37, A4; ☎ 4328-6921; www.movidisc-web.com.ar; 3rd fl, Diagonal Roque Sáenz Peña 868, Microcentro) offers private transportation and day-tours in vans fully equipped for wheelchair users. If you're taking a tour with another agency, Movidisc can provide transportation alone, provided you ask your tour company to arrange it with Movidisc.

Online, check out the following:

Access-able Travel Source (www.access -able.com)

accesible.com (www.accesible.com.ar)

Mobility International (www.miusa.org)

>INDEX

See also separate subindexes for Drink (p173), Eat (p174), Play (p174), See (p175) and Shop (p176).

A

Abasto 108
accommodations 136-7
    farm stays 146
afternoon tea 97
air travel 160-1
Alfonsín, Raúl 154
ambulance services 165
antiques 73-4, 75
architecture 149
art 147
    festivals 24-5
    galleries 60, 147, *see also*
        See subindex
art, folk 72
arteBA 24-5
artisan fairs 15, 21, 73, 96
ATMs 167

B

Barrio Chino 130, 133
Barrio Norte 90-101, **91**
bars 142, *see also* Drink
    subindex
Basílica de Nuestra Señora
    del Pilar 92
beef 22, 132
Belgrano 128-33, **129**
Biblioteca Nacional 92-3
billiards 59-60
boat travel 161-2
books 157
bookstores 57, 58, 95-6

000 map pages

Borges, Jorge Luis 68, 157
Bosques de Palermo 107
bus travel 163
business hours 164, *see also*
    inside front cover

C

Cabildo de Buenos Aires 38
cafes 14, *see also* Drink subindex
Caminito 18, 86
canoeing 148
Carnaval 24
cartoneros 155
Casa de la Cultura 38
Casa FOA 26
Casa Rosada 38
Catedral Metropolitana 38
cathedrals, *see* See subindex
cell phones 168
Cementerio de la Recoleta
    11, 93
Centro Cultural Borges 39
Centro Cultural de los
    Artistas 88
Centro Cultural Recoleta 93
children, travel with 150
Chinatown 130, 133
Chinese New Year 24
churches, *see* See subindex
circuses 82
Ciudad Cultural Konex 108
climate change 162
clubbing 122, 143, *see*
    also Play subindex
Congreso 52-61, **53**
Cortázar, Julio 157

Costanera Norte 122
costs, *see inside front cover*
credit cards 167
Creamfields Buenos Aires 26
currency 167, *see also inside*
    front cover
cycling tours 168

D

dance clubs 122, 143, *see*
    also Play subindex
desaparecidos 152
design
    exhibitions 26
    markets 15, 21, 73, 96
dinner reservations 111
Dirty War 152, 153-4
disabilities, travelers with 169
drinking, *see also* Drink
    subindex
    Barrio Norte 99
    Belgrano 132
    Congreso 58-9
    Las Cañitas 132
    Microcentro 43-4
    Palermo Viejo 122-4
    Puerto Madero 50-1
    Recoleta 99
    Retiro 68-9
    San Telmo 79-82
    Tribunales 58-9
drinks
    mate 106
    tea 97
    wine 16
Duhalde, Eduardo 154

E

economy 152, 155
Edificio Kavanagh 64
El Molino 54
El Museo Fortabat 48
El Zanjón de Granados 72
electricity 165
emergencies 165, *see also inside front cover*
empanadas 88
environmental issues 155-6
estancias 146
events 23-6
exchange rates, *see inside front cover*

F

Faena Hotel + Universe 46, 136-7
Falkland Islands war 154
farm stay accommodations 146
fashion 145, *see also* Shop subindex
    festivals 25
Feria de Artesanos de Plaza Francia 96
Feria de Mataderos 21, 58
Feria del Libro 24
Feria San Pedro Telmo 73
Festival Internacional de Cine Independiente 24
festivals 23-6
Fiesta del Inmigrante 26
filete 72
films 158
film festivals 24
fire services 165
Firpo, Luis Angel 11
Floralis Genérica 94
folk art 72

folk music 19, 58, 111, 127, 158
food 141, *see also* Eat subindex, Shop subindex
    Barrio Norte 98-9
    beef 22, 132
    Belgrano 131
    Congreso 57-8
    empanadas 88
    ice cream 109
    La Boca 88
    Las Cañitas 131
    Microcentro 42-3
    Palermo 109-10
    Palermo Viejo 118-22
    Puerto Madero 49-50
    Recoleta 98-9
    reservations 111
    Retiro 66-8
    San Telmo 76-9
    Tribunales 57-8
free activities 31
fútbol 12, 89, 148
Fundación Proa 18, 86

G

Galería Güemes 39
Galerías Pacífico 40-1
galleries 60, 147, *see also* See subindex
Gardel, Carlos 25, 56, 108, 138
gardens 20, 49, 64, 72, 104, 107
gay travelers 26, 144
government 154-5

H

Hernández, José 157
Hipódromo Argentino 133
history 152-5
holidays 165
horse shows 24

I

ice cream 109
Iglesia Santa Catalina 39
internet resources 166
itineraries 29-31

J

Jardín Botánico Carlos Thays 104
Jardín Japonés 104
Jardín Zoológico 104
jazz music 101, 111
jewelry, *see* Shop subindex

K

kayaking 48
Kirchner, Cristina Fernández de 152, 155
Kirchner, Nestor 152, 154, 155

L

La Boca 18, 84-9, **85**
La Bombonera 12, 89
La Feria de Mataderos 21
La Rural 25, 104
La Semana del Arte en Buenos Aires 25
language 166-7
    slang 80
Las Cañitas 128-33, **129**
Las Madres de Plaza de Mayo 17, 40, 58, 152
leather 41, 66, 97, 117-8
lesbian travelers 26, 144
literature 157
Lunfardo 80

M

Macri, Mauricio 154
magazines 167
MALBA 105
malls 40-1, 97, 107, 108, 109

Manzana de las Luces 39-40
Maradona, Diego 89
Marcha del Orgullo Gay 26
markets 15, 21, 58, 73, 75, 96
Martín, Benito Quinquela 86, 159
Mataderos 58
mate 106
meat 22, 132
Ménem, Carlos 154
Mercado de San Telmo 75
Microcentro 36-45, **37**
milongas 10, 45, 60, 61, 125, 127
mobile phones 168
money 164-5, 167
Monumento a los Españoles 105
Monumento a Sarmiento 105
Museo Casa Carlos Gardel 108
Museo de Arte Español 130
Museo de Arte Popular José Hernández 105-6
Museo de Artes Plásticas Eduardo Sívori 106
Museo de Bellas Artes de la Boca Benito Quinquela Martín 86
Museo de la Inmigración 48
Museo de la Pasión Boquense 86-8
Museo Etnográfico 40
Museo Evita 106
Museo Fragata Sarmiento 48

Museo Histórico Nacional 72
Museo Municipal de Arte Hispanoamericano Isaac Fernández Blanco 64
Museo Nacional de Arte Decorativo 106-7
Museo Nacional de Bellas Artes 94
Museo Xul Solar 94
museums 147, *see also* See subindex
music 140, 158-9, *see also* Play subindex, tango festivals 26
    folk 19, 58, 111, 127, 158
    jazz 101, 111

N
ND/Ateneo 69
newspapers 167
nightclubs 122, 143, *see also* Play subindex
Nuestros Caballos 24

O
Obelisco 40
Once 108
opening hours 164, *see also inside front cover*

P
Palacio Barolo 54
Palacio de las Aguas Corrientes 54
Palacio del Congreso 54
Palais de Glace 95
Palermo 102-11, **103**
Palermo Viejo 112-27, **114-15**
Palermo Woods 107
parks 20, 49, 64, 72, 104, 107

Parque 3 de Febrero 107
Parque Lezama 72
parrillas 22, *see also* Eat subindex
passports 162
peñas 19, 58, 111, 127
Perón, Eva 'Evita' 11, 93, 106, 153
Perón, Juan 153
Piazzolla, Astor 139
planning 30, 164
plastic surgery 156
Plaza de Mayo 17, 40
Plaza del Congreso 54-6
Plaza Dorrego 73
Plaza San Martín 64
police 165
politics 154-5
pollution 155-6
polo 26, 148
pride marches 26
Puerto Madero 46-51, **47**

R
Recoleta 90-101, **91**
religion 156
remises 164
Reserva Ecológica Costanera Sur 49
restaurants, *see* food, Eat subindex
Retiro 62-9, **63**

S
Sábato, Ernesto 157
San Telmo 13, 70-83, **71**
Sarmiento, Domingo 11
senior travelers 165
shopping, *see also* Shop subindex
    Barrio Norte 95-8
    Belgrano 130-1

000 map pages

Congreso 56-7
La Boca 88
Las Cañitas 130-1
malls 40-1, 97, 107, 108, 109
Microcentro 40-2
Palermo 107-9
Palermo Viejo 113-18
Recoleta 95-8
Retiro 64-6
San Telmo 73-6
Tribunales 56-7
soccer 12, 89, 148
sports 148
Subte 163-4
subway, see Subte

T
tango 10, 138-9
    classes 45, 60, 127
    festival 25
    Gardel, Carlos 25, 56, 108, 138
    halls 45, 60, 61, 125, 127
    shows 59-60, 82, 83
Tango Buenos Aires 25
tax 163
taxis 164
tea 97
Teatro Colón 60
Teatro Nacional Cervantes 61
Teatro San Martín 61
telephone services 168
theater 60, 61, 82, 108, see also Play subindex
tipping 168-9
Torre de los Ingleses 64
tourist information 169
tours 167-8
    shopping 116
train travel 164
Tribunales 52-61, **53**

V
vacations 165
visas 162-3

W
wine 16
    festivals 25
writers' festivals 24

X
Xul Solar, Alejandro 94, 159

Y
Yrigoyen, Hipólito 11
Yupanqui, Atahulapa 159-158

Z
zoos 104

🍸 DRINK

Bars & Clubs
647 79
Bar 6 123
Bar Británico 79
Bar Iberia 58
Bar Plaza Dorrego 79
Bar Seddón 79
Buller Pub & Brewery 99
Carnal 123
Casa Cruz 123
Clásica y Moderna 99
Cruzat Beer House 58-9
Dadá 69
Doppelgänger 80
El Federal 80
El Living 59
Gibraltar 80
Home Hotel 123
Kandi 132
La Cigale 43-4
La Puerta Roja 82
Le Bar 44

Lelé de Troya 123-4
Malas Artes 124
Marriott Plaza Bar 69
Milión 99
Mundo Bizarro 124
Pipí-Cucú 132
Soul Café 132
Sugar 124
Supersoul 132
The Library Lounge 51
Van Koning 132-3
White Bar 51

Cafes
Bar 6 123
Bar Británico 79
Bar Iberia 58
Bar Plaza Dorrego 79
Bar Seddón 79
Café Literario Osvaldo Bayer 58
Café Retiro 68
Café Richmond 43
Café Tortoni 43
Clásica y Moderna 99
El Federal 80
L'Orangerie 97
La Biela 99
La Puerto Rico 44
Las Violetas 44
Malas Artes 124
Mark's Deli 124
Oui Oui 124

Gay & Lesbian Cafes
Pride Café 82

Pubs
Bangalore Pub & Curry House 122
Buller Pub & Brewery 99
Cruzat Beer House 58-9

🍴 EAT

Argentine
788 Food Bar 98
Almacén Secreto 118
Bar Uriarte 118-19
Casa Felix 118
Cumaná 98
Freud y Fahler 120
La Vinería de Gualterio
 Bolívar 77-8
Manolo 78
Museo Evita Restaurante 110
Restó 57
Social Paraíso 121-2
Standard 122
Tomo 1 43

Asian
Cantina Chinatown 133
Comedor Nikkai 76-7
Empire Thai 67
Green Bamboo 120
Irifune 67-8
Little Rose 121
Lotus Neo Thai 133
Moshi Moshi 131
Sipan 68
Sudestada 122

Delis
i Fresh Market 50-1

European
Cluny 120
Ølsen 121

French
Azema Exotic Bistró 118
Brasserie Berry 42

Brasserie Petanque 76
Casa Roca 42
La Bourgogne 98
Le Sud 68

International
Azema Exotic Bistró 118
California Burrito Company 42
El Bistro 50
Gran Bar Danzon 98
Novecento 131-2

Italian
Amici Miei 76
D'Oro 42-3
El Cuartito 57
Filo 67
Il Matterello 88
La Parolaccia del Mare 51

Moroccan
Bereber 119

Organic
Origen 78
Pura Vida 43

Parrillas
Cabaña Las Lilas 49
Don Julio 120
El Desnivel 77
El Establo 66-7
El Obrero 88
Gran Parrilla del Plata 77
La Brigada 77
La Dorita 120-1
La Vieja Rotisería 77
Miranda 121

Peruvian
Sipan 68
Status 57-8

Seafood
Plaza Asturias 57

South American
Mosoq 121

Spanish & Basque
Café San Juan 76
La Vinería de Gualterio
 Bolívar 77-8
Oviedo 98-9
Plaza Asturias 57
Sagardi Euskal Taberna 78-9
Taberna Baska 79

Vegetarian
Artemisia 109
Bio 119-20
Pura Vida 43

⭐ PLAY

Concert & Live Music Venues
Centro Cultural Torquato
 Tasso 82
Ciudad Cultural Konex 108
La Cumparsita 83
La Peña del Colorado 111
La Trastienda 83
Los Cardones 127
Luna Park 45
ND/Ateneo 69
Niceto Club 127
Notorious 101
Teatro Gran Rex 45
Thelonious Club 111

Dance Clubs
Asia de Cuba 51
Bahrein 44-5
Basement Club 101
Big One 45
Caix 122
Club Aráoz 110

000 map pages

Cocoliche 45
Crobar 110-11
Jet 122
Kim y Novak 125
Maluco Beleza 60
Museum 83
Niceto Club 127
Pachá 122
Rouge 122

Gay & Lesbian Bars & Clubs
Bach Bar 124-5
Bulnes Class 110
Glam 101
Sitges 127

Jazz Clubs
Notorious 101
Thelonious Club 111

Sporting Venues
Campo Argentino de Polo de
  Palermo 133
Hipódromo Argentino 133
La Bombonera 12, 89

Tango
36 Billares 59
Bar Sur 82
Centro Cultural Torquato
  Tasso 82
Centro Region Leonesa 61
Confitería Ideal 45
El Beso 60
El Querandí 83
El Viejo Almacén 83
La Cumparsita 83
La Viruta 125
Salon Canning 127

Theater
Circo del Aire 82
Ciudad Cultural Konex 108
Teatro Colón 60

Teatro Nacional Cervantes 61
Teatro San Martín 61

⊙ SEE

Churches & Cathedrals
Basílica de Nuestra Señora
  del Pilar 92
Catedral Metropolitana 38
Iglesia Santa Catalina 39

Museums & Galleries
Braga Menendez Arte
  Contemporaneo 60
Casa de la Cultura 38
Centro Cultural Borges 39
Centro Cultural Recoleta 93
Daniel Abate 94
El Museo Fortabat 48
Floralis Genérica 94
Fundación Proa 86
Isabel Anchorena 94
MALBA 105
Museo Casa Carlos Gardel 108
Museo de Arte Español 130
Museo de Arte Popular José
  Hernández 105-6
Museo de Artes Plásticas
  Eduardo Sívori 106
Museo de Bellas Artes de
  la Boca Benito Quinquela
  Martín 86
Museo de la Pasión Boquense
  86-8
Museo de la Inmigración 48
Museo Etnográfico 40
Museo Evita 106
Museo Fragata Sarmiento 48
Museo Histórico Nacional 72
Museo Municipal de Arte
  Hispanoamericano Isaac
  Fernández Blanco 64

Museo Nacional de Arte
  Decorativo 106-7
Museo Nacional de Bellas
  Artes 94
Museo Xul Solar 94
Ruth Benzacar 60
Zavaleta Lab 60

Notable Buildings &
Monuments
Biblioteca Nacional 92-3
Cabildo de Buenos Aires 38
Casa Rosada 38
Cementerio de la Recoleta
  11, 93
Edificio Kavanagh 64
El Molino 54
El Zanjón de Granados 72
Galería Güemes 39
Manzana de las Luces 39-40
Monumento a los Españoles
  105
Monumento a Sarmiento
  105
Obelisco 40
Palacio Barolo 54
Palacio de las Aguas
  Corrientes 54
Palacio del Congreso 54
Palais de Glace 95
Puente de la Mujer 48-9
Torre de los Ingleses 64

Parks & Gardens
Jardín Botánico Carlos Thays
  104
Jardín Japonés 104
Parque 3 de Febrero 107
Parque Lezama 72
Plaza San Martín 64
Reserva Ecológica Costanera
  Sur 49

Plazas & Streets
Barrio Chino 130
Caminito 18, 86
Plaza del Congreso 54-6
Plaza de Mayo 40
Plaza Dorrego 73

Zoos
Jardín Zoológico 104

🏠 **SHOP**

Antiques
El Buen Orden 74
Gabriel del Campo Anticuario 74
Gil Antigüedades 73-4
HB Antiques 74
Mercado de San Telmo 75

Art
Autoría 64
Centro Cultural de los Artistas 88

Books & Music
Café Literario Osvaldo Bayer 58
El Ateneo Grand Splendid 95-6
Gandhi Galerna 57

Fashion
Ashes of Roses 130
A.Y. Not Dead 95
Calma Chicha 113
Cora Groppo 113-16
DAM 116
Etiqueta Negra 96
Felix 116

Ffiocca 73
Gil Antigüedades 73-4
Hermanos Estebecorena 116
Jeans Makers 109
Juana de Arco 117
Moebius 75
Nadine Zlotogora 117
Pablo Ramírez 75
Puntos en el Espacio 75-6
Rapsodia 118
Tramando 97-8

Food & Wine
0800-Vino 108
Anuva Vinos 130
El Fenix 96
La Cave de la Brigada 74
Ligier 66
Lo de Joaquin Alberdi 117
Tealosophy 97
Valenti 131
Winery 42

Home Decor
airedelsur 95
Autoría 64
Buenos Aires Design 95
Calma Chicha 113
L'Ago 74
Materia Urbana 74
Tramando 97-8

Jewelry
JCB Gems & Carvings 66
Plata Nativa 41

Leather
Casa Lopez 66
El Remanso 66
Humawaca 117

Prüne 41
Qara 117-18
Rossi & Caruso 97

Malls
Alto Palermo 107
El Abasto 108
Galerías Pacífico 40-1
Paseo Alcorta 109
Patio Bullrich 97

Markets
Feria de Artesanos de Plaza Francia 96
Feria de Mataderos 58
Feria San Pedro Telmo 73
Mercado de San Telmo 75

Shoes
28 Sport 113
Corre Lola 130
Darcos Tango 40
Josefina Ferroni 97
Puntos en el Espacio 75-6

Souvenirs & Handicrafts
airedelsur 95
Arte de Pueblos 56
Artesanos de Argentina 73
Centro Cultural de los Artistas 88
Club de Tango 56
Darcos Tango 40
Fundación Silataj 130
JCB Gems & Carvings 66
L'Ago 74
Papelera Palermo 117
Plata Nativa 41
Tierra Adentro 66
Wussman 76